Christian Perspectives on Globalisation: A World United or a World Exploited?

Text copyright © 2013 remains with authors and for the collection with ATF Press.
All rights reserved. Except for any fair dealing permitted under the Copyright Act, no part of this book may be reproduced by any means without prior permission. Inquiries should be made to the publisher.

Interface: A Forum for Theology in the World
Volume 16, Number 1, 2013

Interface is an ecumenical and interdisciplinary journal dealing with issues of a social and cultural nature.

Interface is a refereed journal

Editor in Chief: Hilary Regan, Adelaide
Dr Paul Babie, University of Adelaide, Adelaide
Revd Dr John Capper, MCD University of Divinity, Melbourne
Dr Josephine Laffin, Catholic Theological College/Flinders University, Adelaide
Rev Dr Jeff Silcock, Australian Lutheran College, Adelaide

Advisory Board
Dr Stephen Garner, School of Theology, University of Auckland
Dr Aaron Ghiloni, Trinity Theological College, Brisbane
Dr Philip Kariatlis, St Andrew's Greek Orthodox College, Sydney

Mailing address: *Interface*, PO Box 504, Hindmarsh, SA 5007, Australia.
email. hdregan@atf.org.au

Subscription rates (2013)
Australia: Individual Aus $55   Overseas: Individual and Institutions: Aus $95
             Institutional Aus $85

Interface is published by ATF Theology, an imprint of ATF (Australia) Ltd (ABN 90 116 359 963), and is published in May and October of each year. *Interface* is indexed in the *Australasian Religion Index*.
ISSN 1329-6264

Cover design by Astrid Sengkey
Layout/Artwork by Anna Dimasi

Text Minion Pro Size 11

Published by:

An imprint of the ATF Ltd.
PO Box 504
Hindmarsh, SA 5007
ABN 90 116 359 963
www.atfpress.com

Christian Perspectives on Globalisation:
A World United or a World Exploited?

ATF Theology
Adelaide

2013

Interface Vol 16/2 2013

Table of Contents

Editorial
Peter Price   vii

Being, Wellbeing and Globalisation
Stephen Ames   1

Globalisation and the Moral Crisis in Economics
Bruce Duncan   35

The Globalisation of Theology
John D'Arcy May   64

Contemporary Globalisation and Local Struggles
for Social Justice
Rowan Ireland   81

Globalisation and Christian Education:
Impacts and Responses
Therese & James D'Orsa   101

Global Mission: Consequences for the Marginalised
Robyn Reynolds   117

Ernst Troeltsch on Christianity in a Globalising World
Wes Campbell   130

Contributors   144

Editorial

Peter Price

I remember clearly across fifty years, as though it were last week, being enthralled by the 'Global Village' concept promoted by the Canadian Social Psychologist, Marshall McLuhan. In the introduction to his 1964 book, *Understanding Media*, McLuhan wrote: 'Today, after more than a century of electric technology, we have extended our central nervous system in a global embrace, abolishing both space and time as far as our planet is concerned.'[1] Like many people, though not all gave McLuhan their full respect, I dreamed his poetic vision of a world in which national boundaries might gave way to 'World Citizenship', a world united, as we developed the sense of our global connectedness through even greater 'electric technology' than McLuhan could have imagined back in the 1960's. Who for example could have envisaged in 1964, something as powerful as the Internet facilitating global exchanges? Who would have envisaged in 1964, a global European Union?

The possibilities of globalisation, there at the beginnings of its socio-cultural recognition, seemed to be infinite. Indeed, they seem now to be even more so. This issue of *Interface* investigates some of those possibilities, their fulfillment, their progress or their corruption into something different. It comes from an ecumenical Christian interchange between a group of scholars interested in social policy and its interface with the voice of Christian social justice, the general wellbeing of people, the solidarity of humanity, and the responsibilities of government for the common good.

---

1. *Understanding the Media: The Extensions of Man* (New York: McGraw-Hill, 1964), 3.

Today, all kinds of items pass over national boundaries pretty much without hindrance. Merchandise, money, debt (especially debt), learning, information, media and technology, for example, transcend national borders and flow freely between peoples. Only people themselves seem to find barriers to migration, as 'Border Protection' becomes a national priority to the extent it has become a core political driver in Australian society. The plight of refugees, long ago related in United Nations protocols for good world citizenship, but seemingly too complex to be held accountable by them, has emphasised in bold the fragility of what I term, the 'McLuhan dream'. But it is not the only sign of global fragility in our times. Multi-national exploitation of less mobile, less powerful peoples, most often resulting in burdens of indebtedness, the interest on which often exceeds the national budget for health and other social wellbeing expenditure, has beggared whole peoples, and created growing gaps between rich and poor on a global scale. Some refer to it as the 'trans-nationalisation of poverty'.

But economics is not the only elemental force in the globalisation phenomenon. The possibilities for social development, for cultural exchanges, and the sharing of technological advances in science, health, and education are also endless. On the other side of the coin, the suppression of cultures, especially minority cultures by global neglect or global exploitation is not infrequent even in our own enlightened times.

It would be wrong to ignore the significant blessings of globalisation across these and the many other realities that sit within the complex that we have named 'globalisation'. In this issue of *Interface* we look at many sides of the phenomenon. The authors of the following articles in this journal are board members or associates of the Yarra Institute for Religion and Social Policy. The Yarra Institute is an Ecumenical Christian Research Institute within the University of Divinity, based in Melbourne, Australia. The articles range across some of the current directions and forms of globalisation that contribute to global unity and wellbeing. They cover global economics, education, the value of local cultures and leadership, the global sense of the 'Common Good', and the global solidarity and fundamental dignity of all humanity.

In the first of these articles, Stephen Ames considers human well-being from a Christian perspective based on the belief in our being created in the 'Image and likeness of God', with the profound theological implications of that belief. The Christian perspective is counter-posed against the view of Australian author, David Malouf in his 2011 essay, 'The Happy Life'. Here, amid all the progress that should make humans happy, there is an endemic 'unrest'. Malouf argues that it results from the loss of 'personhood' in the great global connectivity, 'the impersonal world we have created and in which we live so restlessly'. Into this 'unrest' Ames brings the Christian emphasis on Trinity, or God as community, pure relationship, into clear understandings of the personal, essentially relational nature of the human person in God's likeness and the immense dignity that accrues to the human being from that very fact. It is only in close integrity with that likeness can humanity find 'rest'. The implications of these realities of the self in relation for the global community are of the infinite variety.

Ecumenist, John D'Arcy May takes up the theological theme, with a new perspective, looking at how theology itself has forged global connections across a range of faith traditions. John addresses the question of the possibility of a 'World Theology', a collaborative, person-centred approach to relationships between religious faith traditions of various kinds. He wonders how religion might feature in a new world where the 'multi-polar, multi-religious shape of the world has been captured by the term *Globalisation*. The possibility of a global civil society emerging, brings with it the fascinating question, 'what will be the place of religion in it?' John resurrects in an inter-connected world, the possibility of a world theology to discover that place. In this context, he rightly questions what he calls the 'secularisation thesis' in the light of the growth of world Islam, the immense interest in faiths like Buddhism that transcend traditional national boundaries, and the growing concern with indigenous religion in various forms. It is a thesis needing revision

Bruce Duncan and Rowan Ireland move us into the economic and socio-cultural elements of globalisation. Bruce commences with the so-called 'Global Financial Crisis', arguing that it has arisen from systemic and viral market corruptions facilitated by the collapse of moral standards in the quest for exponential growth and 'ever-expanding' wealth. Such unrealistic expectations, based on supposed beneficial social impacts accruing through wealth at the top end of world economic agencies, in fact involve dangerous externalities such as labour force distortions, global poverty, and damage to the natural environment that supports human life. Far from absolving economic agents from 'moral responsibility' about the consequences of their actions', Bruce argues that the true market economy can only operate fully when it is underpinned by carefully conserved moral principles like integrity and the pursuit of the common good. It is here that the churches have a message to voice. Rowan, on the other hand expands into the broader social and cultural implications of the often-contradictory impacts of global connectivity. He examines the threat-benefit contradictions on economics, politics and culture in the context of a particular local struggle for social justice. His core case-study of a residents' association in a Brazilian shantytown illuminates his view of the integrity of the local community and its culture in a globalised world of such vast connectivity that sometimes the biggest and loudest voices drown out the small, rendering them 'voiceless' and unable to have their concerns noticed. Alternately, such connections also have the capacity to inform and draw resources from, a wider world able to relate with and support such local struggles for justice.

Robyn Reynolds and Therese and Jim D'Orsa look at the core issue of this series, through what might be described as a missiological lens. Robyn's essay is particularly of this persuasion. It resumes, as a starting-point the themes from earlier essays in this journal, considering that globalisation of religion and contact with the diversity of religion through globalisation have caused the emergence of a new approach to Christian mission. Robyn argues that growing awareness that 'all cultures and religions can proclaim and witness to the betterment of humanity', becoming in the process a manifestation of divine presence in the world. From this inclusive view, Robyn argues that the 'new' theology of Mission enters into dialogue between religious traditions and their surrounding cultures to engage in the reconciliation of peoples. Christian mission theology finds itself 'alongside the marginalised, the poor of the earth and the earth itself'. Such an approach cries out for total inclusiveness on a global stage, drawing out and hearing the voices of those previously marginalised in a patriarchal, colonial society, especially women and indigenous peoples.

The D'Orsas on the other hand, consider the impact of globalisation on the human ability to make meaning from our experience of the world around us. They argue that a fundamental task of Christian education is to help young people make sense of their life-world so that they may pursue truth and develop a personal relationship with God as revealed in Jesus. How they understand their life-world and locate themselves within it depends on how they make sense of it. The processes of so doing are strongly impacted by globalisation. Sociological research into the worldview of young people provides insight into the ways in which they see the world which reflects the impact globalisation is having on their meaning-making processes. This has important implications for the work of Christian educators in guiding young people in a 'brave new world'.

The final essay stands alone in some ways, and yet is strongly connected by the theological threads running through all the essays. It takes its theme from the work of Ernst Troeltsch (1865 – 1923), German theologian and philosopher of religion, perhaps best known for his work, *The Social Teaching of the Christian Churches*, published in English in 1931. Though he preceded the latter half of the twentieth century's understanding of globalisation by a significant period, it is clear that he encountered what Wes Campbell refers to as the 'relativising' impacts of peoples' wider contact with cultures besides western civilisation, and the same impact on western Christianity from contact with world religions. Starting from the view that globalisation is 'both a concept and a lived experience resulting from the mutual contact between societies around the globe', Wes examines Troeltsch's search for a 'secure footing for Christian faith in a globalised setting among the plurality of cultures'. It was a search that for Troeltsch was a needed response to his growing sense that the 'absolute truth' of Christianity demanded re-examination when placed over against other cultures and other religions. It is this response that Wes explores.

In this era of rapidly escalating change, the search for continuing meaning, values, openness to dialogical understanding, global hospitality and furtherance of human dignity, the bringing of a deeply Christian perspective to this matter of globalisation is part of a growing conversation that must take us into a space where the full advantages of it, and the minimisation of its harmful impacts become not just possibility, but conscious reality.

Globalisation and the realisation of its full potential present a challenge for the social, cultural, economic and political, as well as the Christian forces in our societies throughout the world.

There is so much that remains on the threshold of possibility, the influence of financial markets and the world bank, the development and conservation of rich and diverse cultures, the resilience of individual communities, the growing gap between the rich and the poor at both individual and national levels, the burning question of intergenerational solidarity and responsibility, and the conservation of the natural ecologies of our environment. There is such a long way to go. Globalisation has become a much more complex and often paradoxical reality than the simple *Global Village* notion as a 'coming together' of peoples through advanced communication technologies. It has now become a matter of exchange across the broad spectrum of human existence. I am not sure just how McLuhan might feel about the directions in which the 'global village' has drawn us, but it has not lost any of its possibilities, nor its allure.

Being, Wellbeing and Globalisation

Stephen Ames

When I think about discussions of 'wellbeing', in either the objective or subjective senses,[1] I wonder what notion of 'being', is presupposed. I think the idea of 'wellbeing' calls for ontological[2] clarification. On the other hand 'globalisation' is often lauded for promoting the good of all or bewailed for its failures. Globalisation has some connection with 'wellbeing' or its discontents. These two lines of thought lead me to expect a connection between 'globalisation' and 'being'. 'Globalisation' also calls for ontological clarification. This paper is a sketch of such a clarification.

Of course discussions of wellbeing and globalization without this clarification are very valuable.[3] I am interested, however, in the further value of bringing to light what ontological presuppositions are carried by these discussions.[4] I know that not everyone will see

---

1. A similar distinction between 'prosperity' and 'happiness' is used in Tim Jackson, *Prosperity Without Growth, Economics for a Finite Planet* (London, Earthscan, 2011), 36.
2. In brief, an 'ontology' is a theory of what there is. The clarification I am interested in concerns the assumptions about what kind of world it is in which we live that are present in discussions of wellbeing and globalisation.
3. For example: Abdalla, S, Mahoney, S, Marks, N, Michaelson, J, Seaford, C, Stoll, L, and Thomson, S, *Measuring our Progress: The Power of Well-being* (New Economics Foundation, 2011), go to: http://www.orcacomputer.com/isqols/content/NEWS/measuring_our_progress_webReady.pdf); Diener, E, and, Seligman, MEP, 'Beyond Money, Toward and Economy of Well-Being', in *Psychological Sciences in the Public Interest*, 5/1 (2004): 1–31; Langmore, J, *To Firmer Ground: Restoring Hope in Australia* (Sydney NSW: UNSW Press, 2007).
4. Two other examples of my engaging in 'ontological clarification' are Stephen Ames, *Cosmology and the Metaphysics of Inquiry*, (PhD thesis, University of Melbourne 2006, unpublished); 'Resonances and Dissonances between Church and Society' in, *Church and Society* (Adelaide, SA: ATF Press, 2004): 142–185.

the need for such a clarification. I have therefore chosen to discuss a very widely read and very well received 2011 essay, 'The Happy Life', by David Malouf. I show how the essay allows us to see clearly the need for an 'ontological clarification', though the term is not mentioned nor the clarification provided in that essay. I also initiate the desired clarification from two angles – one through what I glean from Malouf and one from a Christian standpoint.

David Malouf on the Happy Life

David Malouf is an internationally renowned Australian author.[5] Malouf's essay on the 'Happy Life'[6] begins by drawing our attention to Solzhenitsyn's, *One Day in the Life of Ivan Denisovich*, to the prisoner Shukhov on a day when he goes off to sleep completely content because the 'day had gone by without a single cloud—almost a happy day' (2).

For most of history only an elite have had favourable social and material conditions providing the luxury of going beyond rare momentary happiness to 'considering what happiness of a more settled kind might be' (2). The classical tradition from Seneca to Aristotle and Plato affirmed self-containment and self-reliance, and this is still echoed in the seventeeth century poem by Sir Henry Wootton, 'Character of a Happy Life'. (3) This presents the image of man who holds together the active and contemplative poles of life, who amidst all temptations without and within, remains, 'Lord of himself, though not of lands, and having nothing, he hath all' (4). Happiness for such a man is in retiring to his own quiet room alone (5).

---

5. David Malouf won the inaugural Australia-Asia Literary Award in 2008 and was awarded the Neustadt International Prize for Literature in 2000. His 1993 novel *Remembering Babylon* won the International IMPAC Dublin Literary Award in 1996 and he was shortlisted for the Booker Prize in 1994. In 1998 David Malouf was invited to deliver the Boyer Lectures on ABC Radio. These six lectures '. . . explore how living in one hemisphere and inheriting our culture from another affects who we are and the sort of world we make for ourselves in Australia.' The Boyer Lectures are delivered each year by a prominent Australian who is invited '. . . to present their ideas, and the results of his or her work and thinking on major social, scientific or cultural issues'.
6. David Malouf, 'The Happy Life, The Search for Contentment in the Modern World', in *Quarterly Essay*, 41 (2011): 1–55. All page references to this essay will be in the body of the text.

The contrast to our own time in developed societies is that happiness is something we all aspire to whatever our position in society and this as a right. Malouf offers the sharpest contrast between us and all previous history with the following comment.

> The question that arises is not so much, 'How shall we live if we want to be happy?' but how is it, when the chief sources of human *un*happiness, of misery and wretchedness, have largely been removed from our lives—large scale social injustice, famine, plague and other diseases, the near-certainty of an early death—that happiness still eludes so many of us? What is it in us or in the world we have created that continues to hold us back? (8).

Malouf thinks of this dissatisfaction as the 'latest version of what Plato's *Protagoras* identifies as "unrest"' (41), the distinctive character of human beings created by Epimetheus and equipped with gifts stolen by Prometheus from the gods. Since humankind is naturally restless it undermines any possibility of finding happiness as a settled state of being.

Malouf identifies numerous factors informing our natural 'unrest'. We have a new vision of the earth seen from the moon, a planet, fragile, complex, and unique. From that vantage point we are invisible even inconsequential (44). If our planet is dying it will be disastrous for us but only another 'moment' in the history of the planet. Life on the planet is an accident and so are we (43).

The various schools of the classical tradition were in no doubt as to the 'importance of the Self as the purest agency of being and its need to be protected from the distractions, the temptations and dispersive busyness of things' (45). We are not so sure. We tell a different story about life in which the Self of the classical tradition 'does not quite fit' (45). We speak about DNA, evolution, and the brain described by neuroscience.

While our awareness has expanded beyond the scale and reach of our physical bodies—in the direction of the infinitely large and the infinitely small—we have become more aware of our bodies (45). We are even obsessed with our bodies as our basic sense of self and with the care of our bodies using all of the resources provided by science and the market. Freed from guilt about sensual pleasure we know our bodies are for enjoyment and for display, an advertisement to ourselves and for others, of an 'otherwise vague and unimaginable self' (46). And this vague sense of self is 'validated' by being attractive, and its presence and vigour is reaffirmed in a healthy orgasm. Though the sin of sensuality is gone, the new shame is failure of either performance or presentation. We may not be afraid of the 'finality and nothingness of death' but we are afraid of the trials of extended longevity, where we lack control of our bodies and minds (46).

'One consequence of the 'Epimetheus version of our condition history is unfinished, forever in process; endless because our needs are endless' (48). Technology has helped meet those needs and the problems it creates, but will it continue to do so? Technology has a life of its own and our brains are not evolving fast enough to keep up with the accelerating rate of innovation (48). We feel that our life is not safely in hand, that the future we are facing is possibly darker (41) than all the optimists have believed, following the Marquis de Condorcet (d 1794), who relatively recently turned our attention away from the once authoritative past to the progressive, unprecedented and unlimited future. 'Time had a new shape' (27). So did authority.

Within the expanded scales of space and time, energy and matter we have acquired a new sensibility in which the small and large, the local and global are interconnected in:

> . . . global Environment . . . global Security, global Culture, and in an age of large-scale management, the global Economy with its Market Forces, its International Trading Agreements, the IMF, the World Bank—a global power with its own mystique and the authority to demand instant obedience and absolute belief (44).

As for this economy keeping us all

> connected, in its mysterious way, by laws that *do* exist, the experts assure us, though they cannot agree on what they are—it is too impersonal, too implacable for us to live comfortably with, or even to catch hold of and defy. (49).

It is this want of the personal, the dominance of the impersonal that Malouf several times (48, 49, 51, 55) refers to as the root of what unsettles us.

> What most alarms us in our contemporary world, what unsettles us and scares us, is the extent to which the forces that shape our lives are no longer personal—they no longer know us; and to the extent that we know nothing of them—cannot put a face to them, cannot find in them anything we recognise as human—we cannot deal with them. We feel we are in the coils of an invisible monster, that cannot be grasped or wrestled with (55).

At the end of the essay Malouf returns to Shukov, who can deal with his situation, which is within the limits of his grasp, if not his control. Not a settled state of being of contentment and rest but as 'a kind of happiness he can make do with from one day to the next' (55).

I have only given a glimpse of this very engaging essay. It is clear that Malouf offers an account of wellbeing both in an objective sense as the good life which is free of many of the causes of human misery and unhappiness and in the subjective sense of the aspiration to a personal contentment and happiness as the right of all human beings, even if in the modest form of momentary happiness day by day. Malouf traces these two senses of wellbeing to the American Declaration of Life, Liberty and the pursuit of Happiness as the inherent rights of every human being given by their creator (9). While he places no weight on the reference to the Creator, he sees these rights as addressing the natural, social and personal levels of existence (10).

By way of the intended clarification, what ontology does Malouf espouse in this account of wellbeing and globalisation? Two answers can be obtained from the essay. One is a naturalism based on the natural sciences and technology. This is shown in Malouf's privileging the story we now tell about the evolution of life, DNA, and neuroscience in which there is no place for the 'Self'—that pure agency of being - of the classical tradition.[7] We see it also in his entertaining the prospect

---

7. This is ontological naturalism as distinct from epistemic and methodological

of the evolution of the brain as we adapt to the new conditions brought about by technological innovations and their accelerated entrée into our lives. Malouf sees here the possibility of a 'new form of "being"' in which the Ego is by-passed through an overload that is the equivalent of intense physical activity, with the release of endorphins producing euphoria (23). There we experience the 'rush of wellbeing . . . an awareness of intense personal presence' (24).

On the other hand the second answer is suggested in his clear view that what is so disturbing for 'us' is the impersonal and implacable character of the world in which we now live. In this perspective technology has a life of its own and the 'agency' in us (24) that has allowed us to adapt to it is now not keeping up with the rate of innovation. Whereas the classical tradition prescribed philosophy as the cure for 'unrest' (21), the latter is now the cure for 'something quite opposite but equally close and pervasive: the fear of inactivity, of stillness . . . in an extended and unendurable *silence*' (22). For Malouf it is as if Pascal's terror at the 'eternal silence of infinite space' has found a new form. The 'unrest' of hyper connectivity is our cure. Sitting still, alone in a room is impossible—whereas once it was thought to be the source of happiness.

What is surprising is that the suggestive second answer does not motivate a question about the impersonal construal of reality (the naturalism and technological innovation of the first answer) that forms the now taken for granted world in which we live so restlessly, which Malouf believes serves as a 'fix' for handling the fear of an unendurable silence. No critique is pursued, despite the repeated reference to the alienating and 'impersonal' character of the world we have fashioned for ourselves. This second answer offers Malouf no starting point or route to explore an alternative ontology. For Malouf and presumably for the many people who have appreciated and applauded his essay, the 'Self' as the pure agency of being in the classical tradition is not a starting point. But is there no alternative?

Malouf's view is that the restless character of human beings is due to some fundamental lack, which we live with even as we use the 'gifts' fabulously stolen by Prometheus from the gods. These are the 'interior and godlike qualities' of imagination and invention,

---

naturalism. It is the view that what there is, is what the natural sciences say there is, ultimately physics, or complex configurations of the same.

which human beings will have to develop in themselves, along with other prior qualities such as 'curiosity . . . and a flair for observation, for seeing below the surface and beyond the recording of singular phenomena' (18, 19). Malouf doesn't examine these 'gifts' to see whether they point to a richer ontology. This is surprising firstly given that Prometheus steals the gifts from the gods. Secondly, Malouf's remarks on the 'best known proposition from classical Greek thought' which is Protagoras' 'Man is the measure of all things'. According to Malouf Protagoras was declaring,

> that humanity is at the centre of the system we call Creation, and that Man, with his particular qualities of reason, the power of speech, the capacity to name and make and remake, is the point from which we must start in any inquiry into the laws of the system, any exploration we might set out upon into the nature of knowing and being. But he was also pointing out the importance to our investigations—of how one thing is related to another—of measure, or as we are more likely to call it, proportion (51).

I entirely approve of this exploration and its starting point.[8] It seems obvious that Malouf does follow Protagoras' advice with regard to the starting point—'Man'. But he does not follow Protagoras with regard to the focus of the exploration, which for Malouf is not the nature of 'knowing and being' but of human happiness. There is another surprise here. The classical tradition prescribed philosophy as the cure for 'unrest'. Philosophy was expected to help the individual, who by

> learning to distinguish between real and unreal desires and fears, frees himself from the 'busyness' of a world that is endlessly pushing for the new, the more; from engagement, attachment, dependency; from what, as we have seen in Montaigne, in being external takes us away from the sufficiency of the self (21).

---

8. See Bernard Lonergan, *Insight* (London: Darton, Longman and Todd, 1958) for an example of such an inquiry.

The tradition offers a critical stance, which appeals to a certain understanding of the 'Self'. Remove that understanding of the Self and what approach is available for the distinguishing between real and unreal desires and fears? One possible answer is via the construal of what is 'Man' in the wake of innovative technology with a life of its own, with most of us struggling to evolve quickly enough to keep up, especially with digital technology and all its chatter within the fundamentally impersonal global economy. Adaptations to this construal of reality are 'real' and what is not is 'unreal'. We could even take this version of 'Man' as the starting point for Protagoras' inquiry into 'knowing and being'. But that would be superficial. After all, even Malouf points to something deeper in what I have identified as the suggestion of a second answer to the question about the ontology he espouses in his account of wellbeing and globalisation.

This achieves one aim of this essay, which is to show how Malouf helps us see the need for an 'ontological clarification' of the impersonal world we have created in which we live so restlessly, of the different story we now tell about ourselves in which the old account of the Self does not fit, and of momentary, unsettled happiness for which it seems we must settle. The starting point and impetus for this ontological clarification has something to do with our sense being persons. But what? Malouf does not say.

A Christian view of Wellbeing and Globalisation

I turn now to sketch an ontological clarification[9] of 'wellbeing' and 'globalisation' from a Christian standpoint.[10] I begin with two well-known biblical themes. One is the assertion that humankind was created in the image and likeness of God.[11] The other concerns the worship of idols. According to Psalm 115, idols have eyes but cannot see, feet but cannot walk etc. and those who worship them become

---

9. This may be thought to overlook my stated approval of Protagoras' project of making 'Man' the starting point for an inquiry into knowing and being. If it is not confusion surely it sets up a conflict between faith and reason. But this would be premature. For Christians both faith and reason come from God. Ultimately there cannot be any conflict between the two and there will only seem to be conflict if one or both is distorted.
10. For an impressive and for some a contentious exposition of these matters see the 2009 Encyclical Letter of Pope Benedict XVI, *Caritas in Veritate*.
11. Genesis 1:26–28.

like them.[12] They degrade their humanity. They acquire a way of being human in the image of a lesser god. From these two themes it follows that enjoying well being depends on the extent to which our way of being human goes with or against the grain of our being created in the image of God. On this basis, the crucial element for enjoying wellbeing is to do with what we worship.[13]

This is a second order understanding of well being. It becomes specific depending on what we say about the God who created human kind and what follows from this as the corresponding way of being human 'in the image of God', which is then properly called 'well being'.

Christ, the image of the invisible God[14]
The Christian understanding of God came from the church's extended reflection on the 'new reality' that had come into the world through Jesus, to which the whole Bible gives inspired testimony. The God so revealed was recognised by Christians as the God who had spoken in many and various ways[15] through the Law and the Prophets of Israel, whose reality was intimated in ordinary experience.[16] This 'new reality' is the foretaste and anticipation of the coming of the reign of God in glory, the only future that is coming—fullness of imperishable life which will flood the whole universe.[17] It shone through the Spirit-empowered person of the Son incarnate in Jesus, his teaching, his mighty works, his forgiving sins, and his fellowship

---

12. Other examples of this theme are Ps 135, Jeremiah, 2:4.
13. Lest this last point seem a too narrowly religious focus for the well being of *human kind*, collectively and individually, the Old Testament makes clear that there is no authentic worship without justice being done to widows, orphans, the poor and strangers. The point is intrinsic to worship, since righteousness and justice are the foundations of God's reign (Psalm 89:14; Isaiah 58). Our actions and attitudes manifest what has worth for us. It is shown in how we spend time, money and energy. This is our daily 'wor(th)ship'. We shall see even from the first chapter of Genesis how wide is the ambit of divine justice. This is not too narrow a focus for 'well being'.
14. Colossians 1:15.
15. Hebrews 1:1.
16. For example, Psalm 19; Romans 1:19-20; Acts 17:28.
17. You may remember the story in the Gospel of Mark of the woman who breaks a flask of pure nard to wash Jesus' feet before he dies. The whole house was filled with the perfume from the broken flask. John 12:1-7. For Christians it is a sign of what is to come.

with the spiritually outcast and marginalised. It shone through his being raised from the dead and was only then seen in his crucifixion. It was received in the new experience of the Spirit among his disciples following his death and resurrection. The heart of this new reality was indicated in Jesus' words, 'No one knows the Son except the Father and no one knows the Father except the Son and those to whom the Son chooses to reveal him'.[18]

The divine economy
This new revelation of God in Christ brought to light the 'mysteries of God', the divine plan (oikonomia, economy) for the whole world,[19] which God is everywhere at work to bring to its consummation, when all things in heaven and earth will be transformed by being united 'in Christ', when 'God will be all in all',[20] when the whole creation is drawn into the life of the Triune God. This is the end to which human history is heading, through all the resonances and dissonances between this divine economy and human beings' exploring and exploiting all the creative powers of the 'original blessing'. These creative powers are being discovered, in and through all the distortions due to idolatry, and just there the grace of God continues to meet us to bring us on our way in a turbulent history.[21]

The trinitarian understanding of God
The distinctively Christian understanding of God is expressed in the two dogmas of the Incarnation and the Trinity. A crucial matter in each dogma concerns the understanding of the term 'person'. It was Christian theologians who made a historically original and extended exploration of the meaning of this term.[22]

In the early centuries of our common era Christian theologians turned to Greek thought to help articulate the gospel of Jesus the

---

18. Matthew 11:27. St. John's Gospel is the extended reflection on this new reality.
19. 1 Corinthians 4:1; Ephesians 1:9–10; 3:9–11; Colossians 1:24–29; Matthew 25:34. See also, Raymond Brown, *The Semitic Background to the Term 'Mystery' in the New Testament*, (Philadelphia: Fortress, 1968); Stephen Long, *The Divine Economy: Theology and the Market* (London: Routledge, 2000).
20. 1 Corinthians 15:28.
21. See Bernard Lonergan, 'Healing and Creating in History', in *A Third Collection*, Frederick Crowe, editor (New York: Paulist Press, 1985).
22. Rolnick, PA, *Person, Grace and God* (Grand Rapids: Eerdmans, 2007).

Messiah in ways that could make sense to their Hellenistic audience.[23] Platonism and neo-Platonism initially seemed a most promising resource. Everyone involved was aware that various aspects of Christian belief were at risk of distortion by this medium. Charles Taylor identifies a number of points of tension.[24]

(1) In the pagan view the body was ruled by the soul, but in Palestine of Jesus' time this view, if present, was secondary to the question of the state and direction of the heart. (2) This leads to a new significance for history. 'The relation of the human heart to God was a story of falling away and returning.'[25] This was the central narrative of human history, which had an end. For Christians the end was a gathering of the whole story, of all the stories, not just the arrival at an end state. (3) The stories gathered into God's eternity entail the significance of individuals 'whose identities are worked out in these stories'. By contrast the different ways of access to the eternal for Plotinus and Aristotle means loss of individuality. (4) The stories that are the central narrative of the history give a new place to contingency. This includes responding to the neighbour who accidently crosses my path. History is not the implementation of the rigidly scripted divine plan of the Stoics but a resourceful responsiveness on God's part, come what may, to bring history to its end—a telos not a terminus. (5) With all these factors there is also the place of the emotions. For Christianity, rather than the highest human condition being purged of emotion, they are part of our relation to the highest being. Taylor[26] quotes Martha Nussbaum' discussion of Augustine:

> We hear sighs of longing and groans of profound desolation. We hear love songs composed in anguish, as the singers' heart strains upward in desire. We hear of a hunger that cannot be satisfied, of a thirst that torments, of the taste of a lover's body that kindles inexpressible longing. We hear of an opening that longs for penetration, of a burning fire that ignites the body

---

23. Charles Taylor, *A Secular Age* (Cambridge Ma: Belknap, Harvard University Press, 2007), 275.
24. Taylor, *A Secular Age*, 275–279.
25. Taylor, *A Secular Age*, 276.
26. Taylor, *A Secular Age*, 278.

and the heart. All of these are images of profound erotic passion and all of them are images of Christian love.[27]

The problem was that the educated elite of Hellenism conceived of God as 'apatheia', beyond emotion. But this was in tension with the Christian identification of Christ with God and with the pain filled death of Christ.[28] (6) According to Taylor all these factors only make sense in the context of the Christian belief that God is a personal being, not just as agency, but also as capable of communion. The theological struggle was to make sense of the Scriptural witness to the Father, the Son and the Spirit and its equally powerful witness that God is one. What follows is an impossibly brief summary of some of key themes in the development of this understanding of God.

At its core the Arian controversy was about the understanding of God to be used in interpreting the Bible. Arius (256–336), a Christian presbyter from Alexandria in Egypt took the understanding of the being (*ousia*) of God from Greek thinking. This guided his interpretation of the Bible. God had no contact with creation and so Jesus could not be God incarnate. There had to be a difference in being between Jesus and God. Athanasius (298–373), the bishop of Alexandria, allowed the Bible to inform his understanding of God, which led to a new understanding of being. The Father and the Son have the same being (*homoousios*). Likewise the Spirit was of the same being as the Father and the Son.

Following Athanasius a crucial step was taken by the Cappadocian theologians.[29] Whereas *ousia* and *hypostasis* were synonyms in Greek philosophy for 'substance', 'essence', these theologians distinguished between *ousia* and *hypostasis*. 'God is one *ousia*, ("substance", "essence", or "being") equally and fully expressed in three *hypostases*, the Father, Son and Spirit'.[30] This innovation initiated Christianity's distinctive elaboration of the meaning of *hypostasis*, still an

---

27. Martha Nussbaum, *Upheavals of Thought* (Cambridge: Cambridge University Press, 2000), 528.
28. See the discussion of this contested theme in recent theology by Christiaan Mostert, 'God's Transcendence and Compassion', in *Pacifica*, 24/2 (June 2011):172-189.
29. Basil (330-379), Gregory of Nazianzus (329-389) and Basil's younger brother Gregory of Nyssa (335-395).
30. Rolnick, *Person, Grace and God*,18.

ontological term, to refer to 'person' (rather than 'prosopon' from the mask used in the theatre) and as an entirely new thought, was irreducible to *ousia*. The divine substance has no reality 'prior' to or apart from the distinctions between the three persons. These distinctions are eternal, and are ontologically primary.

While each *hypostasis* has 'common qualities, like infinity, being uncreated . . . each *hypostasis* can also be distinguished by origin, relatedness, and how it is known by creatures'.[31] The three 'persons' are mutually defined in their uniqueness and otherness; they ontologically co-inhere in their dynamic unity, their perichoresis ('dance'), their communion. These themes mark out the distinctively Christian understanding of being: to be is to be in communion.[32] Lastly, the sovereignty or 'monarche' of God is to be thought of as belonging not just to the Father (contra the Cappadocians) but also to the triune God (following Athanasius).[33]

The biblical revolution—the fundamental order is personal
Taylor places this theological achievement in a context of a struggle,

> the whole package (1) – (6), arose out of a struggle, that of Patristic theology with earlier ideas of an impersonal order, be it that which identified the highest with an idea . . . or with Plotinus' One or with a God whose defining characteristic was apatheia. Now in the modern era we see this package challenged by new understandings of order, running at one end of the spectrum from Deism, to modern atheist materialism at the other.[34]

Taylor explains that the 'pull towards the impersonal pole of this continuum'[35] from the eighteenth century on, was due to the ways the human condition was understood in terms of an impersonal order that ultimately has its roots in the rise of modern science, both for

---

31. Rolnick, *Person, Grace and God*,19.
32. Zizioulas, *Communion and Otherness: Further Studies in Personhood and the Church*, edited by P McPartlan (New York: T&T Clark, 2006).
33. Kevin Giles, *The Trinity and Subordinationism: The Doctrine of God and the Contemporary Gender Debate* (Illinois: Intervarsity Press, 2002), 40–43.
34. Taylor, *A Secular Age*, 279.
35. Taylor, *A Secular Age*, 280.

deism and for modern atheistic materialism. This move was further understood as superseding the earlier idea of the fundamental personal order, which was then seen as belonging to a bygone era.

Colin Gunton[36] points out the further move towards the impersonal in Descartes defining the human person in terms of an individual non-spatial mind and a spatial body which 'it is very difficult, even for God, we might say, to join together'.[37] Cambridge Platonists were anxious about Descartes' philosophy which included reducing animals to machines. Given all that animals could do it seemed to open the way to treating human beings as machines. This fear was fulfilled by de La Mettrie's (1709–1751) book, *Machine Man*,[38] and more latterly with evolution, cognitive sciences, and neuroscience proposing a completely naturalistic account of the human mind.

For Gunton, the Cartesian tradition, even in its naturalistic form is the dominant modern tradition about persons. However he also points to a minor tradition represented by the Scottish philosopher John MacMurray's second volume of his 1953/4 Gifford Lectures,[39] with a crucial link to this later development of the relational view of persons, possibly being nineteenth century Scottish philosopher Sir William Hamilton influenced by Calvin in the sixteenth century. What is also of interest is the parallel between MacMurray and the writings of Richard of St Victor in the eleventh century, who continues the Christian trinitarian reflection on the understanding of 'person'. Gunton observes that here the idea of God does not fit Feuerbach's maxim: theology is really anthropology in disguise.[40]

Cartesian influences on theologians meant that the distinctively Christian view of 'person', both divine and human receded. The recovery of Trinitarian understanding of God initiated in twentieth century in Protestant (Karl Bath) and Catholic theology (Karl Rahner), and massively developed [41] subsequently, is a prerequisite

---

36. Colin Gunton, *The Promise of Trinitarian Theology* (Edinburgh: T&T Clark, 1991), chapter 5.
37. Gunton, *The Promise of the Trinity*, 87.
38. Julien Offrey de La Mettrie, *Machine Man and Other Writings*, translated and edited by Ann Thomson (Cambridge: Cambridge University Press, 1996).
39. John MacMurray, *Persons in Relation* (London: Faber & Faber, 1961).
40. Gunton, *The Promise of the Trinity*, 93.
41. Among many, many books I mention the following in addition to those already

for a Christian view of 'wellbeing'. This is also the recovery of the Patristic struggle for a fundamentally personal order rather than the prevailing view of a fundamentally impersonal order. The challenge for theology is to show how this fundamentally personal order, theologically understood, can robustly and convincingly incorporate the large impersonal scientific story of the universe, including the evolution of life and human life in particular.

Created in the 'image of God'
Christian theology asserts that the whole universe has been freely created by God *ex nihilo* for a purpose, as a free sovereign act, which God is everywhere at work to fulfill. Humankind is created in the image and likeness of God.[42] This 'original blessing' has been understood in three ways: ontologically, relationally and functionally.[43] The 'ontological' concerns *who* we are—persons— and *what* we are—the human nature we all share. In a Christian account of the being of human beings the person is ontologically

---

noted, Karl Bath, *Church Dogmatics*, volume 1, edited by G Bromiley, and T Torrence (London: T&T Clark, 2009); Karl Rahner, *The Trinity*, translated by Joseph Donceel index and glossary by Catherine LaCugna (New York: Crossroad, 1997); Catherine LaCugna, *God For Us: The Trinity and Christian Life* (San Francisco: Harper, 1993); Alan Torrance, *Persons in Communion: An Essay in Trinitarian Description and Human Participation, with Special Reference to Volume One of Karl Barth's Church Dogmatics* (Edinburgh: T&T Clark, 1996); Colin Gunton, *Father, Son & Holy Spirit: Toward A Fully Trinitarian Theology* (Edinburgh, T&T Clark, 2003).

42. This is a classic site for the principled holding together of faith and reason— here in the form of the natural sciences. Galileo's 'two books' principle offers a path to holding together the theological assertions and the scientific discoveries in cosmology and in the evolution of life on earth. See for example, Brendan Purcell, *From Big Bang to Big Mystery: Human Origins in the Light of Creation and Evolution* (Dublin: Veritas, 2011); Rolston Holmes III, *The Three Big Bangs: Matter-Energy, Life, Mind* (New York: Columbia University, 2010); Denis Edwards, *How God Acts: Creation, Redemption and Special Divine Action* (Adelaide: ATF Press, 2010); Stephen Ames, 'Why Would God Use Evolution?', in *Darwin and Interfaith Perspectives,* edited by Jacques Arnould OP (Adelaide: ATF Press, 2010), 105–128. On the other hand the application of the principle is popularly trivialised by 'stretching' the biblical text over the latest piece of science; for example the claim that vegetation and animals appear in Genesis 1 in the same order as they do according to evolution.

43. Stephen Garner, 'Image bearing Cyborgs?' in *Theology and the Body,* edited by Stephen Garner (Adelaide: ATF Press, 2011), 19.

prior. We are each unique, embodied persons ontologically oriented for communion with God and with one another.[44] This orientation is the basis for the claim made famous by Augustine, that our hearts are restless until they rest in God.

The communion with one another may take many forms but of special importance is the assertion that humankind is created in the image of God as 'male and female'.[45] Together men and women share the 'original blessing'. This is a remarkable counter-cultural assertion.

The 'relational', concerns our being drawn and called into personal communion with God and with one another, and into an analogous relationship with the earth by which we are dynamically embodied. Thus our relationship with each other is to be in the 'image of God' marked by otherness, equality and dynamic unity. This relational aspect of the 'original blessing' is being discovered in a long unfinished, historically contested process from early evolutionary post hominid ancestors right up to today.

The 'functional' concerns humankind being given 'dominium', sovereign power to be used *together* as good stewards of the earth for all humankind now and into the future.[46] By this power we are to

---

44. This embodiment is different from the idea of the person as an immortal soul imprisoned in the body, also from any idea of the body as secondary to the person, and from the idea of the person reduced to being wholly a function of the body. In addition to the references before the previous one, some other useful discussions of these matters are in *In Search of the Soul: Four Views of the Mind Body Problem*, edited by Joel Green and Stuart Palmer (Illinois: Intervarsity Press, 2005); and Nancy Murphy, *Bodies and Souls or Spirited Bodies?* (New York: Cambridge University Press, 2006); Karl Rahner, *Foundations of Christian Faith* (London: Darton Longman and Todd, 1978), 178-187.
45. For some Christians this entails defining same sex relationships as unnatural and against the God given purpose of gender and sexuality. This includes denying biology as having any contribution to the idea of what is natural. For example Max Champion, 'Nihilism and Nature, Bonhoeffer's "Theology of the Body" and the Homosexuality Debate', in *Bonhoeffer Down Under*, edited by Gordon Preece and Ian Packer (Adelaide: ATF Press, 2012), 105–126. I recognise the force but not the finality of these considerations, which I cannot discuss here. I want to acknowledge that same sex, exclusive, life-long relationships are truly loving relationships and deserve to be honoured as such. Indeed the failure to give this honour is not theologically innocent.
46. This is a radical theme since such power was attributed only to rulers, whether in Egypt or in Babylon or the other nations, which Israel eventually wanted to emulate (1 Samuel). It is also radical in that land does not belong by right to the 'crown' but to the people as God's stewards of the land. This is a stewardship

do justice to our being embodied persons, to our utter dependence on the life-giving earth and to the fair share in the blessings of the good earth God has given, which is thus the right of all people. This is the wide ambit of divine justice for created life and human life in particular. Genesis is already a prophetic vision of the life of *humankind* and so of life in what we would call 'global' terms.[47]

Given what has just been noted about 'male and female' as the form in which humankind is created in the 'image of God', the actual relations between men and women should be characterized by otherness, equality, unity—especially in marriage but also in all aspects of their relating. This is a radical Biblical position not least because of the shared dignity of men and women and because of the shared exercise of 'dominium'.[48]

---

that is not an exclusive ownership of land but a trust in which all have a share, exercised in particular communities. In the ordinary exchanges between communities and individuals the stewardship ought not be nor merely sold (see the story of Naboth's vineyard), nor redefined by force of arms or legal fiction of declaring a different kind of sovereignty as was done by Governor Philip on the 26th of January 1788 at Sydney Cove in the name of George III, King of England. This has many implications for a theological view of indigenous communities in their relation to the land.

47. This is not to invoke our global economy, which is not strictly speaking an 'economy' (see below) and does not intend a fair share of God's gift of the earth in order that all may live a good life. Hundreds of millions of people have been lifted out of poverty by the expansion of a global economy over the last forty years. But that is hardly the main purpose of the economy.

48. This is in some tension with St. Paul in 1 Corinthians 11:2–16, which denies that women are created in the image of God and the 'shame' in 1 Corinthians 14:35 should a woman speak in church. The latter may be thought to also be in tension with Galatians 3:28 where 'in Christ' there is no 'male and female'. The distinction is hardly denied as indicated in Paul's discussion in 1 Corinthians 6. But rather the way of living out the distinctions is now set free for the new humanity inaugurated in Christ. What will this be? Surely it is not the continuation of the old cultural practices of placing the man over the woman. Surely the guide should be that in Christ God's intention from the beginning should now be enacted in the world as was the parallel overcoming in Christ of the distinction between Jew and Gentile. The further parallel is Jesus' discussion of divorce and marriage, quoting from Genesis, where the latter has the truly countercultural note that it is the man who would leave his father and mother and be joined to his wife. Kevin Giles has brought out the way the understanding of the relation between men and women as involving the submission of a women to men under the doctrine of 'headship' is so important that it can inform the (mis)understanding of the Trinity. Kevin Giles, *The Trinity*

This threefold 'original blessing' of humankind is God's gift to the whole creation since it is through the incarnation of the divine Son as a human being that the divine purpose for the whole creation will be realized.

The unconditional worth of created life
Creation and its promised consummation, through the incarnation of the Son, the image of the invisible God, deepens the meaning of human kind being created in the 'image of God'. The incarnation shows us the true image of God in whose 'image' we are created. It shows human nature was and is always oriented to the incarnation of God and more importantly that God was always oriented to the incarnation.[49] This demonstrates the God-given worth and dignity of creation and of human beings in particular.

Human dignity and worth is also indicated by the 'sovereign' powers (dominium) entrusted to human kind to ensure that the earth can go on being life-producing now and into the future, and, as we shall see, within this trust to ensure that the earth's abundant good is wisely distributed for the common good of humankind to whom it is given.

The deepest demonstration of the worth to God of the whole creation and of humankind in particular is the costly means God has used to redeem us from all idolatrous ways of being human, which together represent a path that has no future, because it has no place in the future that is finally coming from God. Through the incarnate Son the 'new reality' of the reign of God has come into the world. The

---

and Subordinationism.
49. I stand in the tradition that takes the incarnation as the inner meaning of creation rather than being a consequence of the fall. A history of this theological tradition in the church has been given by Brooke Westcott, 'The Gospel of Creation', in, *The Epistles of St John* (London: Macmillan, 1883), 273–315. The Rev Dr Barry Marshall first introduced me to this idea when I arrived as an Anglican ordinand at Trinity College in Melbourne in 1962. I had little idea of what it meant except that the idea evoked in me a sense of standing on the edge of a large, but strange space I had never known before. Drawing on Karl Rahner, Dennis Edwards has recently deployed this incarnational theme to speak about the one divine action in Christ from creation to consummation. Denis Edwards, 'Resurrection and the Costs of Evolution: A Dialogue with Rahner on Noninterventionist Theology', in *From Resurrection to Return, Perspectives from Theology and Science on Christian Eschatology*, edited by James Haire, Chris Ledger, and Stephen Pickard (Adelaide: ATF Press, 2007), 120.

world could not bear this 'new reality' so it rejected Jesus, even to the point of crucifying him. But this was not the last word. Just when we had thereby seemingly slammed shut the door that God had opened, the 'new reality' triumphed. Jesus remained open to his Father even in the extremity of his violent death. By the Spirit the Father raised Jesus to glory, to vindicate him and so to keep open the possibility of everyone sharing the divine life, indeed the whole created universe. This opening of the divine life to the whole creation is the costly love of the triune God, a cost felt to the uttermost depths of God.

This is good news because we were created in the image of God, who came in human form, at such a cost, to open entrée into the life of God for which we were created and to do so from within our world. This is what we are worth to God. We might use the words of the old marriage service, to imagine hearing the incarnate God saying to us: 'with my body I thee worship'. For the 'new reality' that has come into the world through Jesus is a foretaste of the ultimate marriage of heaven and earth.[50] This is the love of God for each and all of God's creatures, which God always intended for the whole creation. One way of summing up this good news of the vulnerable and invincible God is provided by this prayer.[51]

> Father, our Saviour, you sent Jesus your Son into the world of sin and delivered him up to death for us. Kindle in our hearts the same love with which he loved his own until the end, who lives and reigns with you and the Holy Spirit, one God now and forever.

Rulers and the divinely given power to humankind
From Genesis this 'sovereign' power is to be exercised by human beings over the earth but not over each other. There is no inherent hierarchy among human beings. Where 'sovereign' power is exercised by kings or other leaders, it is in no way to weaken or deprive people of this shared dignity of having God-given power and responsibility for the ongoing life of humankind. It is to be exercised in the image and likeness of the triune God who created this life-producing universe, not in the image of a death-dealing monstrous idol.

---

50. Revelation 21.
51. Based on the prayer after the psalms in Evening Prayer for Thursdays, from *A Prayer Book for Australia* (Broughton Books, 1995), 441.

The image of 'monstrous' rule is shown in Daniel 7 in the rule of Antiochus IV Epiphanes, and in Revelation 17 and 18, against Rome, especially the merchants who trade in every kind of commodity including human beings. There are many other historical examples. This monstrous rule is contrasted to the coming of the humane reign of the living God.

The Bible has a continuing caution about human 'kings' compared to the reign of God, a caution present all the way from Samuel to Jesus. It finds powerful expression in the conversation between Pilate and Jesus in John's Gospel, and in Jesus' words in the Synoptic Gospels about the 'great men', the so-called benefactors of the world, whose leadership is not to be followed by Jesus' disciples. The caution is maintained by remembering Jesus' word to render to Caesar the things that are Caesar's and to God the things that are God's; by holding together Romans 13 and the recollection that contra St Paul's words it was those who were a terror to good, who wielded 'the sword' that put Jesus to death; by recalling the judgment against 'Babylon' and its rulers in the Book of Revelation and the fact that there are good rulers—David, Josiah, Cyrus, the king in Psalm 72—which presumably is why Revelation 21:26 can envisage the kings of the earth with all their glory entering the New Jerusalem.

The priority of personal relationships

To speak of being created in the image of the triune God is to emphasise the priority of personal relationships, in which the dignity and worth of human beings is acknowledged, which are therefore trustworthy, whether one to one or in community, and this evokes the vision of a trustworthy community of communities of all human beings. Elsewhere Scripture says we now see as in a 'glass darkly', but then we will see 'face to face'. Even now the embodied, face-to-face character of human life, which God is everywhere at work to strengthen, is to be a sign of the glory that is coming.[52] Of course it must be said that humankind is on a long, contested historical journey towards embodying 'globally' the reality of being created in the image of this God.

---

52. The more obvious implications of this have to do with the way we handle our politics, the way the institution makes decisions about individuals, the way we handle conflicts between individuals and groups, the ways we can be more accountable to one another that are constructive, even life giving, the quality of our speaking to and about one another, especially when the 'other' is absent.

The more abstract ordering of society, in the division of labour, in the state and other institutions and organisations, which we establish, may still be in the 'image of God' by serving not subverting the good of persons in relationships. The principles of participation and subsidiarity made central to Catholic social teaching help ensure people are not deprived of the exercise of this God-given power to take responsibility for themselves and their families, to help define and promote the common good of humankind and to hold accountable those who exercise this power on their behalf.

The priority of the personal is vulnerable to the enormous scope of 'dominium'—sovereign power—as these God-given human powers continue to be discovered and their discovery drives human history. Yet such power is only one aspect of being created in the image of God. Our being created as persons has ontological priority. This does not mean the disavowal of power.[53] It does mean we will all need to grow as persons, which means as persons in relation to God, to ourselves, to each other and to the world God gives us, in order not to be taken over by the fruits of these powers gaining a life of their own and we ending up being the narcissistic slaves to 'the works of our hands'. According to the Bible this is idolatry—again—the undermining of our true worth and our true interests.

The ambiguity of human life
As already noted the distortion of the 'original blessing' comes from the worship of idols and the effect of this worship is to dehumanize—we acquire a false way of being human in the image of a lesser god. We are caught in degrading ways of being human. We live a lie. But note, as far as the Bible is concerned the 'original blessing' has not been withdrawn by God. The created being of human beings is in tension with our acquired way of being human. Our living is therefore ambiguous, both drawing out and drawing on God's gift and so manifesting much that is good, that even 'feels good' to us, yet is refracted in the humanly created medium of living 'with and against the grain'.

---

53. This must be affirmed against the uncritical interpretation of Jesus as weak and powerless and the supposed disavowal of power by various post-modern lines of thought. Jesus never relinquished his authority and his integrity even in the extremity of his suffering and death. I would like to see all that Foucault said about power and knowledge applied to his own writings.

By contrast to the worship of idols, we are addressed by the two great commandments: You shall love the Lord your God with all your heart and soul and mind and strength and your neighbor as yourself.[54] God commands and so authorizes us to have access to our full humanity in relation to God, to our neighbor and to ourselves. This stands *with* the 'original blessing' but stands *against* the many distortions that deny one or more aspects of the 'original blessing', as these distortions are pursued in the name of a lesser god or gods or 'higher principles'.

These distortions are the various negations of the original blessing, understood ontologically, relationally and functionally. The distortions therefore include: espousing an impoverished ontology that cannot do justice to the reality of being created as persons who are the image of God on earth; blocking the development or worse promoting the degradation of the personal and interpersonal realities of human life; and the many abuses of power, especially depriving people of their God-given power and responsibility. The worship of lesser gods always entails the degradation, the loss, and therefore the sacrifice of human life, whether or not 'human sacrifices' are offered.[55]

Thank God this oppression cannot utterly exclude the possibility of an uprising by those who are oppressed. This is because, according to Scripture, God has not removed the 'original blessing' from humankind. This ontology ensures the contradictions carried by the distortions will eventually be felt, understood and challenged, albeit under particular historical conditions, in different ways and with various results, including the possibility of a reversal of the process of oppression not just the replacement of one form by another.[56]

The point is that we only know how and how far we have fallen short of the mark, when the mark has been revealed. We only know how and how much we have adjusted to our lack of health (wellbeing) when we meet a truly healthy person. There are and have been many contenders for the standpoint from which this knowledge is gained. They are at risk of installing another round of oppression because

---

54. Mark 12: 28–34.
55. See Jeremiah 19:4–6; 2Kings 17:17; Leviticus 18:21.
56. See Lonergan's discussion of Individual, Group and General Bias, and its reversal, Lonergan, *Insight*, 218–242.

the worship of a lesser god is maintained and therewith the sacrifice of human life in some form. The life, death and resurrection of Jesus breaks this cycle by making present the 'new reality' of the reign of God in him and through him.[57] As the Son incarnate Jesus discloses true human life by disclosing the reality of God as triune, who is no idol. This is the God who desires mercy not sacrifice, forgiveness not revenge, in whose image human kind has been created, who alone calls forth our full humanity together, who is the ontological ground of our wellbeing.

Considering Malouf's Essay in the Light of this Christian Standpoint

Malouf's reflections on The Happy Life are yet another testimony to how far science and technology have pervaded our way of living and thus our understanding of ourselves, our social world. The overall discussion so far allows us to ask the following questions.

On the one hand, is Malouf's essay symptomatic of the unfinished adaptation to the impersonal scientific view of the physical universe, now taken to be the way things are fundamentally, and to the scientifically and technologically informed global economic and social conditions? Is it simply that we are we still learning to adapt our 'selves' to a completely naturalistic view of the world? On the other hand is Malouf's discomfort with this impersonal order symptomatic of a lost cultural connection with a sense of the divine personal order that from a Christian standpoint is fundamental to the whole created universe, within which human persons can be truly at home?

Is the cultural transformation by science, technology and the market wholly a gain to which we must adapt because it is a better adaptation to reality, as in the first question, or, as in the second question, does it involve a loss that is to be resisted because it

---

57. Here I would begin to make a connection to some aspects of the work of anthropologist René Girard, specifically his anthropological argument that the many similarities between the Gospels and the myths of many different cultures is contradicted by the extraordinary dissimilarity viz. that the story is told from the standpoint of the scape goat victim, rather than the standpoint of the victimisers. See, for example, Rene Girard, *Things Hidden Since the Foundation of the World* (Stanford: Stanford University Press, 1987), Book II.

conduces to a profoundly impersonal world view that misconstrues the being and the well being of human beings, and so misconstrues reality?

The questions move us further towards another kind of ontological clarification—what kind of world is it in which we live and move and have our being? The personal theological ontology and ontological naturalism offer two different answers. What follows are at least two ways to pursue the clarification.

One approach, which I will just indicate, is a philosophical requirement to test the adequacy of the respective ontologies. Any proposed ontology must lead to and not prevent an adequate account of human beings. For example it must enable and not prevent an adequate account of human inquiry (shown vividly in the natural sciences), including how human inquirers have come into existence on this planet. If on the contrary it prevented such an account the ontology would undermine its own claim to knowledge. My claim, which I will not defend here, is that naturalism does not meet this requirement, whereas the personal theological ontology does. The first part of the claim assumes there are things about human inquiry which can be shown in principle to resist being completely naturalized.[58] The human person is not reducible to nature, when 'nature' is understood via the natural sciences. This verges on heresy in the contemporary intellectual climate. There are other examples besides human inquiry where the human person resists being completely naturalized.[59] The second part of the claim presupposes that the fundamentally personal order can robustly and convincingly incorporate the large impersonal scientific story of the universe, including the evolution of life and human life in particular. This assumes the earlier claim that faith and reason are not fundamentally in conflict.[60] Of special importance is identifying what it is about

---

58. Support for this view may be found in John Haught, *Is Nature Enough: Meaning and Truth in the Age of Science* (Cambridge: Cambridge University Press, 2009); Michael Polanyi, *Personal Knowledge: Towards a Post-critical Philosophy* (London: Routledge & Kegan Paul, 1958), and in Lonergan, *Insight*, chapter 19; R Scott Smith, *Naturalism and Our Knowledge of Reality: Testing Religious Truth-Claims* (London: Ashgate, 2012).

59. Charles Taylor, 'The Self in Moral Space' Chapter 2 in his, *Sources of the Self: The Making of the Modern Identity* (Cambridge: Cambridge University Press, 1994), 2.

60. Many would claim that the problem of evil, especially the problem of natural evil renders impossible any reconciliation between faith and reason. My response is

the large scientific story that requires it to be incorporated into any larger story. One place I would point to is the above claim that human inquiry, especially scientific inquiry, resists being completely naturalised.

Another way to test these two ontologies draws on what Malouf says about how Christianity views human happiness and human 'unrest'. Let us consider how these are illuminated by the Christian standpoint presented above.

Is Christian 'happiness' only post-mortem?
Malouf says that when 'Christianity offered its adherents happiness it was a reward either for good works or faith, in the next world'(14).[61] He contrasts this to the American Declaration of Independence which declares the pursuit of happiness to be one of the natural rights of human beings intended by their Creator 'in the New World here and now' (14). Rather than placing any weight on this 'religious rhetoric', Malouf says the outward political, administrative and architectural form of the new Republic were based on 'pagan' Rome (14). Of course pagan Rome had its own religious rhetoric. Christian rhetoric was quite different, with notable effect, as we shall see below.

I disagree with Malouf's claim that Christianity offered only happiness in the next world, not in the here and now of this world, especially in the context of the Roman Empire. As discussed above Christian eschatology is about a present and future reality. The reign of God announced and enacted by Jesus is a foretaste of the still greater good that is coming.

The disturbing reality of the reign of God is shown in many ways, for example in the Beatitudes[62] and parables of Jesus as well as the fact of his being crucified and raised from the dead, followed by the new experience of God's Spirit poured into the hearts of all who received the good news of Christ. Was this a private 'spiritual' matter for the early church? Hardly, since Jesus was publicly crucified by the Roman governor and Christians were persecuted as 'atheists'

---

  indicated in Ames, 'Why would God use Evolution?' in *Darwin and Evolution, Interfaith Perspectives,* edited by Jacques Arnould (Adelaide: ATF Press, 2010)..
61. To be fair, Malouf was not aiming to give an exposition of the Christian view of wellbeing. But the one-liner represents a common view, which hardly does justice to Christianity for all its historical ambiguities.
62. Matthew 5:1–12.

who did not worship the imperial gods. This new, disturbing reality had other effects as Eastern Orthodox theologian, Dr David B Hart comments.

> Occasional attempts have been made by scholars in recent years to suggest that the paganism of the late Roman empire was marked by a kind of 'philanthropy' comparable in kind, or even in scope, to the charity practiced by the Christians, but nothing could be further from the truth. Pagan cult was never more tolerant than its tolerance—without any qualms of conscience—of poverty, disease, starvation, and homelessness; of gladiatorial spectacle, crucifixion, the exposure of unwanted infants, or the public slaughter of war captives or criminals on festive occasions; of indeed almost every imaginable form of tyranny, injustice, depravity or cruelty. The sects of the Roman world simply made no connection between religious piety and anything resembling a developed social morality . . . [nothing] like a religious obligation to care for the suffering, feed the hungry, or visit prisoners . . . The old and new faiths represented two essentially different incompatible visions of the sacred order and of the human good . . . The old gods did not—and by their nature could not—inspire the building of hospitals and alms-houses, or make feeding the hungry and clothing the naked a path to spiritual enlightenment or foster any coherent concept of a dignity intrinsic to every human soul; they could never have taught their human charges to think of charity as the highest virtues or as the way to union with the divine.[63]

In the light of the kind of God revealed in Christ, Christianity pursued an ontological clarification of the understanding of God and of the kind of world in which we live and the new way of being human to which we are called by the triune God. It also must be said that due to its many compromises with 'the spirit of the age' it

---

63. DB Hart, *Atheist Delusions: The Christian Revolution and Its Fashionable Enemies* (New Haven: Yale University Press, 2009), 121–124.

took Christianity a long time to realise the radical implications of this clarification with regard to slavery and with regard to women and therefore, still be realised, with regard to men.

The theological significance of our unrest
For a Christian view of 'unrest' Malouf cites two poems, 'The Pulley' and the 'Collar' from George Herbert, a seventeenth century Anglican priest and poet. Together they show us God creating humankind with many gifts (including all the so-called 'gifts' Prometheus had to steal from the gods) save 'rest', in order that we all may find our rest in God, rather than in nature. This 'rest' is attained by giving full consent to God as Lord. Malouf comments on this human consent to God: 'the soul is caught by surprise, a sudden flash of illumination, in a spontaneous yielding of individual consciousness to the finality of Faith' (22). Malouf proceeds to contrast this view of 'unrest' with his own view that our hyper activity today is the cure for the fear of stillness and silence. Whence this fear? For Malouf it is as if Pascal's terror at the 'eternal silence of infinite space' has found a new form. The 'eternal silence' means that contra Psalm 19, the heavens never had declared the glory of God. Pascal's terror was from being alone, not in a room but in an infinite universe.

The Christian standpoint says we are restless until we find our rest in God.[64] In what way is our restlessness to do with our not finding God? We may answer this by again considering idolatry, which in a secularist society is largely unrecognised. I would say that every culture has its cult, even a secularist culture. The cult defines (supposedly) what is ultimately real and of value and it tells how we may live in touch with that ultimate. What is the 'ultimate' that our culture inculcates in each of us? On a daily basis in our culture it is the techno-sciences that tell us what is real and it is the market that tells us what is of value, that is, what is of value to the market

---

[64] I would be careful how I generalized on this point. In conversation with Buddhist friends I have found much agreement about how to live each day. They had no fear of silence and stillness. Compassion is central. One point of difference arose with regard to silence and the sense of life as a mystery that is beyond all thought, all distinctions. The difference was whether it is possible for us to be addressed by the mystery beyond all distinctions. For a Christian, even if the answer received in conversation is 'no', might not this mystery be an intimation of God incognito?

according to the *golden rule—those who have the gold make the rules*. In tension with this is the claim that privately family and friends are most important and also that publically the 'fair go' for all is a key Australian value. Recently, Steve Jobs was the most prominent carrier of this double message.

The still deeper message from the techno-sciences is that there is no ultimate purpose to the universe, and so there is no ultimate value written into the fabric of the universe. The move from purposeless to godless follows. Furthermore the techno-sciences assure us that the personal is produced from fundamentally impersonal natural processes. This construal of reality becomes deeply taken for granted.

Promoting the desire for an ever expanding global economy
I suggest this underlying nihilism has helped promote the ever expanding global economy to become, ironically, a functional replacement for cultural loss of God. Under the sway of this vast idolatrous 'construal of reality' human beings remain inherently restless because the way of life and the underlying world view means they largely cannot not find their rest with God. This is another implication of the 'original blessing' not being removed by God. This restlessness is socially exacerbated for all the reasons Malouf identifies (see above). Then by (mis)interpreting the restlessness as a finite need that can be met by consumption of material goods it is possible to socially and economically turn people into 'consumers' who literally can never have enough, without really knowing why.[65] This is a pre-condition for an ever growing economy.

Under the *golden rule* the first rule is 'make more gold'. As time goes by this becomes not just a common sense means to a better life, but an end in itself. This is what Aristotle described as 'chrematistics', and was taken up much later by Karl Marx and Max Weber.[66] This is the art of gaining wealth for its own sake and is therefore without limit. Aristotle distinguishes this from 'economics' (*oikonomike*), the art of gaining wealth to manage a household and has its limits in maintaining the way of life of that household. Surely chrematistics

---

65. One view is that children in our society are so transformed before they reach pre-school—a view expressed by Hugh MacKay in a private conversation.
66. See the discussion in Michael Eldred, *Social Ontology, Recasting Political Philosophy through the Phenomenology of Whoness* (Frankfurt, ontos/verlag, 2008), 85-121.

finds its most powerful expression two and half thousand years later in the so-called global 'economy'.

The *golden rule* easily leads to demanding an increased return on capital invested and this can be achieved by increasing the amount returned in the financial 'cycle' of the investment-and-the return of money, typically by variously reducing costs, especially labour costs. It can also be achieved by diminishing the time intervals of these 'cycles' and of course having the 'cycles' run 24/7. As the dominant 'cycle' in our society it is the dominant measure of time. Hence life seems to accelerate.[67] There is no rest.

The cultural surrogate for God

As Malouf also recognises this economy has taken the place once occupied by the gods or fate or, using a phrase from the Bible, we could say that functionally the global economy is now that within which we 'live and move and have our being'[68] rather than God. The economy does the 'god job'. It defines reality and value. It defines time. It has its *golden rule* and its two great 'commandments': you can have value if you add value (as a producer); you can get value if you pay for it (as a consumer).[69] Thus it forms us in its own image and sets up endless competition. It punishes those who resist its rule. It

---

67. See, Michael Eldred, 'The Digital Dissolution of Being' in, *Left Curve*, 34 (2010): 112–118. See also Cliff Hooker's discussion of the societal change engine that has been developing since the Renaissance, in Cliff Hooker, 'Between Formalism and Anarchy: A Reasonable Middle Way', in *Beyond Reason, essays on the philosophy of Paul Feyerabend*, edited by Gonzalo Munevar (Boston, Dordretch: Kluwer,1991).The argument is that privileging a particular mode of inquiry (empirical inquiry), which emphasised pushing the world and observing what happens, strongly contributed to the development of a particular social form. Through the development of technology (and the market) this mode of inquiry led to the creation of a continually disturbed and changing environment, thereby disadvantaging individuals and communities that practiced refined adaptations to a stable environment, while privileging individuals and communities that had greater adaptability. Indigenous communities were ravaged. The change engine now has a life of its own generating its own contradictions. For a fuller discussion of the social implications of Hooker's work see Ames, 'Resonances and Dissonances between Church and Society', 147–151.
68. Acts 17:28.
69. There is not the slightest hint under this 'rule' that there is any contradiction due to the consumer also being the producer. See, Nicholas Boyle, *Who Are We Now, Christian Humanism and the Global Market from Hegel to Hearney* (Edinburgh: T&T Clark, 1998), 118.

rewards the faithful with 'infinite possibilities' for self-transcendence, which ironically are always tied to most people being producers and consumers. It provides an encompassing purpose, a surrogate for the objective lack of purpose, a purpose that in the context of this economy is 'self-evident', both limitless and measureable. It is an idol worshipped every day. Its voice is heard in those who proclaim its supposedly unquestionable value in the midst of bringing about the conditional and expendable value of everything else drawn into the market.

These effects are reinforced by the way public life is ever intruding into our private lives through the massive effects of high-tech communications bombarding and forming us as restless, hyper autonomous persons, who have only conditional value to the economy. Alas, this is in tension with the claim that privately, family and friends are most important, and also that publically the 'fair go' for all is our key Australian value. These private and public values are held as if they were unconditional. We do see that value come to life especially under the shock of national emergencies, as in the fires in Victoria and the floods in Queensland. Many commentators expressed the wish this could be how we lived all the time. It seems we revert to an older ethic under the shock of disaster, where people can see 'we are all in it together'. It is an unrecognised remnant of cultural formation continuing from an earlier period in our society more informed by Christianity. The task is to renew our culture by inculcating this value in all aspects of our life.

As work demands expand and the pace of living increases, we have to stay more and more on the surface of relationships—you can not go too deep if you are always on the move. And we are all being moved faster and faster to keep up with the demands of an ever growing economy. We are more and more being drawn into an abstract form of relationship, mediated by our technology to an absent other, so that these relationships become predominant compared to bodily face-to-face relationships.[70] The expanding market helps promote this shift and offers 'therapeutic' consumption as a surrogate for the loss this shift entails. By these means the personal is being slowly degraded.

---

70. I am here briefly drawing on aspects of the position developed by people at ARENA over many years. For an introduction to these views, see Sharp, G, 'Sufficient for the Day', in *Arena Magazine*, 115, (December 2011–January 2012).

All this is the cult at the heart of our culture. This is what our culture insinuates into our lives. It drives the operation of a virulent social form that takes over and makes over more and more of life in its terms, including forming us as unencumbered, individual consumers. To borrow a term from political science, it operates *as if* it was 'sovereign power'—that power of which there is none greater. This is a monstrous self-caricature of the 'dominium' given to humankind for the common good. The caricature concentrates more and more wealth in the hands of minorities within and between nations. The UN Millennium Goals languish, as does the Doha round of negotiations[71]. The 'Occupy' movement is the latest initiative to highlight the effect of the increasing discrepancy between rich and poor, within and between nations, under the prevailing economic order.

Going with 'the grain' or living a lie
From a Christian standpoint, human well being arises as our way of living goes with the grain of our being created in the image of the triune God. This is a way of being that gives priority to persons in relation to other persons rather than their being degraded. Enacting this is the work of cultural renewal at the level of its presuppositions about what is real and of value: valuing human persons and our growing as human persons as a distinct mode of being expressed in a range of individual and social practices that ensure we are not overtaken by the hugely powerful impersonal order of our own making, with the threat to the earth on which we depend.

It may be true that 'the poor have never had it so good'. However if you pick a standard low enough anything can look good. A different standard is being offered in this paper. It is given in the Genesis vision of humankind created in the image of God and together given sovereign power over the earth. We are in this together. A glimpse of what this might mean is available in the comparison of nations with a high and low degree of inequality on a range of measures having a high or low degree of social and personal disorders.[72]

---

71. *The Economist*, the 6th of October 2012, letter from six Ambassadors to the WTO.
72. Richard Wilkinson, and, Kate Pickett, *The Spirit Level: Why Greater Equality Makes Societies Stronger* (New York: Bloomsbury Press, 2010).

Yet another glimpse is available by noticing that in the first chapter of Genesis at the point where humankind is created in God's image, all that is said about God is that God has spoken. To go with the grain of being created in the image of this God will mean that every person must find their voice, which is expected to be creative and productive, and must not be silenced. The caricature of the sovereign power given by God to humankind is evident in the way the voices of so many people are unheard or are ignored.

From the Christian standpoint, this account of human beings, of our supposed wellbeing and of the kind of world in which we live, points to a profound mistake. We are living a lie. The mistake involves the ambiguity already noted. The reality of human life in relation to God is being massively contradicted by the vast, idolatrous, construal of reality. Yet this construal takes place by our drawing out and drawing on God-given human power and all the other powers and intricacies of the created world. The scope of these powers is still being discovered as all this proceeds and consequently this manifests much that is good, even 'feels good' to us, yet is refracted in the humanly created medium of living 'with and against the grain'. This 'feel good' factor helps make the contradiction almost invisible.

The Christian standpoint, however, leads to an expectation that the contradiction will become manifest. One form of the contradiction is the denial of the finitude of created life, in the chrematistic aspiration to no-limits and all its effects. The contradiction begins to be felt with the recognition of things going wrong with our way of life and yet resisted because of the proud sense of something good and powerful being enacted and confirmed in all the successes of *our* technologically empowered way of life.

The contradiction is felt through the threat of climate change, where the no-limits of global chrematistics is undermining the natural ecology and economy that sustains life. But there is a deep and widespread resistance to this recognition because it indicates a threat to the roots of the construal of reality and value, and the consequent ways of living, which we have pursued for over 400 years, to which we are so proudly attached. We resist the thought that somehow we have gone astray. It is also manifested in the various forms of slavery which abound in the global economy.[73]

---

73. Roscoe Howell, *Australia and Modern Slavery* (Sydney: NSW, Slavery Links

The contradiction is also manifested in the global financial crisis, at the centre of our global chrematistics. The crisis was brought about by the fantasy of the limitless growth of an asset bubble feeding on itself, as if it truly had a life of its own. The fantasy of this false transcendence escalated as the financial processes became more and more abstracted from the daily life of people it was supposed to serve. Overall the trust between people and society's institutions was even further degraded. The contradiction is also manifested in the prospect of wars fought over limited natural resources as more and more nations and more and more people within nations desire to live like the West. Warfare was Aristotle's third way of gaining wealth. Despite the dominance and the power of this encompassing construal of reality in the so-called global 'economy', its contradictions to the life-sustaining planet and to human life are being recognised, from a variety of standpoints including the one presented here. As a result there are many explorations of what might become an alternative path for living together—proposals for a carbon free economy, the Tobin tax on financial transactions, the rise of Transitional Towns, the moves to make a rich and robust notion of wellbeing direct economic, social and environmental policies,[74] and proposals for a true global 'economy' not driven by ever increasing growth.[75]

The divine economy is a truly human economy
The Christian standpoint promotes this exploration of an alternative, though Christians also have to face up to their attachments to the way things are and their resistance to change. The good news of Christ reveals the divine *economy* for the whole creation and this means the whole creation is to be thought of as a 'household' or an 'ecology'. One indication of this is that the whole physical universe is needed for life even on one planet, without prejudice to whether there is life on other planets. On this planet the divine economy, which includes the possibility of its idolatrous caricature, also includes its redemption, so that the divine purpose for creation will not be thwarted. This is

---

Australia Inc. Pluto Press, 2011).
74. A main theme of Rio + 20, the United Nations Conference on Sustainable Development.
75. For example, Jackson, T, *Prosperity without Growth: Economics for a Finite Planet* (London: Earthscan, 2009).

being worked out historically through the incarnation of the Son, the image of the invisible God, whose Spirit empowered gospel is able to set us free from the power of the vast cultural idol, especially as more people see the effects of worshipping this idol. This will allow the 'original blessing' to emerge more clearly so that human beings may become unambiguously the carriers of the true image of the living God not the degrading image of the idol. Thus we may hope that all the contours of wellbeing and globalization that were elaborated above as implicated in our being created in God's image can be realised.

The effects of the excesses of the idolatrous construal of reality and the resistance provoked by the hidden 'original blessing', conspire together to bring into public awareness a version of the Genesis vision, albeit named in a variety of other ways, but still a sign of the times. The divine economy calls us to ways of living in a community of communities, where the personal has priority, where participation and subsidiarity mark all the exercise of power, whether technological, economic, political, where different *economies*, both local and global, (not a global *chrematistics*!) sustain finite needs, where the earth is truly honoured, where all can now explore the 'height, length, breadth and depth'[76] of the good of the 'original blessing', especially since through Christ this has been opened up to a foretaste of the 'final blessing', the still greater good that is coming, the dynamic life of the triune God who will be 'all in all'. This is a 'telos' not a terminus. This is the life of exquisite movement, with being still as one restful act in the movement, in which everything partial has gone, but paradoxically faith, hope and love abide,[77] since the divine economy introduces us into the inexhaustible, infinite mystery of the living God.

---

76. Ephesians 3:18.
77. 1 Corinthians 13:13.

Globalisation and the Moral Crisis in Economics

Bruce Duncan

Introduction

The Global Financial Crisis has rocked the international economy to its foundations and unleashed a series of crises that continue to churn destructively through markets and national economies. We are in an unprecedented period of economic upheaval which is even more unsettling because the consequences are still unfolding unpredictably. The crisis has exposed the collapse of moral standards which allowed the corruption in markets to become systemic and to spread internationally with astonishing speed. In considering the need for renewed moral standards to rebuild global markets, we need to bear in mind also the urgent threats to the environment and from climate change.

    This chapter argues that the current economic crisis stems from philosophical flaws in much economic theory, particularly as exemplified in recent neoliberal writers, who thought they had discovered the Midas touch of ever-expanding financial wealth. This ideology was purloined by financial and other special interest groups to free themselves from normal moral constraints in order to maximise wealth for shareholders and themselves. They believed that the market absolved them from moral responsibility about the consequences of their activities. These special interests threw hundreds of millions of dollars a year into reshaping social and political views through their right-wing think tanks and media channels.

    There has been much soul-searching among thoughtful economic actors, distressed at the rapid collapse of finance and markets, with the savage consequences resulting in tens of millions of people losing their jobs, millions in the United States losing their homes, many more in developing countries being plunged back into desperate poverty, and widespread anger and resentment taking shape in extreme political reactions.

The philosophical flaws behind this ruthless ideology have been sharply critiqued by leading economic writers, who also warned that unless these moral foundations are repaired, the markets will not just repeat the recent disasters, but will wreak havoc on an even larger scale. Astonishingly, as we here explore, these economists are calling for the renewal of the moral dimensions in our culture and economies.

The economic crisis raises urgent questions about the role of the churches in responding to the turmoil in world markets, especially about how to place economics as a discipline and in practice on a sounder moral foundation. The churches have traditionally been key agencies of value formation in cultures, helping establish frameworks of meaning and a hierarchy of values, but these frameworks have been badly frayed by widespread failures in ethics, by neoliberal ideology and by a secularist cultural environment. The crisis presents a fresh opportunity to establish a new moral framework that can guide globalisation, which confronts us with pressing issues about human wellbeing and the common good, and particularly notions of social justice and social equity.

Globalisation for better or worse

Globalisation is an immensely complex process driven by the increasing intensity of economic relations throughout the world. It has delivered great benefits, increasing productivity, better living standards and material wellbeing for the rapidly growing world population, and lifted hundreds of millions out of the most severe poverty. Yet the processes of globalisation, as we are now acutely aware, are fraught with setbacks and dangers.

As Cardinal Peter Turkson, president of the Pontifical Council for Justice and Peace, said in 2010 that although globalisation had lifted millions of people out of poverty, the Church was deeply 'concerned about the flagrant disregard for human dignity, inequality, poverty, food insecurity, unemployment, social exclusion, violations of religious freedom, and materialism that continue to ravage human communities, with destructive consequences for the future of our planet and for our human family'.[1]

The economists, Nouriel Roubini and Stephen Mihm, wrote in *Crisis Economics* that 'increased inequality has caused a growing malaise and concerns about globalization and free trade'.[2] Entire industries are moving between countries and outsourcing of jobs is causing major disruptions to labour markets in developed countries. They warn of 'far more frequent and virulent crises', particularly because of the speed with which financial capital can move in and out of countries, rendering prices highly volatile and causing financial crises. 'The recent crisis has made it clear that the "Great Instability" may be a better description of the coming era than the "Great Moderation".'[3] They support the role of free markets, but with many others call for reform of the financial and monetary systems with more astute regulation, along with broader safety nets and retraining for working people. All this will require 'more, not less, government'.[4]

Roubini warned in September 2011 that we could be facing a second Great Depression 'if the euro-zone crisis becomes disorderly and leads to a global financial meltdown'.[5]

How could our most sophisticated financial markets and business leaders have plunged the world into such an economic maelstrom? What happened in the discipline of economics, with all the data analysis and computer modelling available to it, to have allowed this to happen, if not actually encouraging it?

The warning signs about the deficient ethics of international finance and markets have long been apparent, and the Global

---

1. Cardinal Peter Kodwo Appiah Turkson, 'The Social Doctrine of Benedict XVI in Caritas in Veritate,' in *Crisis in a Global Economy: Replanning the Journey. Proceedings of the 16th Plenary Session of the Pontifical Academy of Social Sciences 30 April-4 May 2010*, edited by Jose T. Raga and Mary Ann Glendon (Vatican City: Pontifical Academy of Social Sciences, 2011), 50.
2. Nouriel Roubini and Stephen Mihm, *Crisis Economics: A Crash Course in the Future of Finance* (New York: Penguin, 2010), 299.
3. Roubini, *Crisis Economics*, 300.
4. Roubini, *Crisis Economics*, 301.
5. Nouriel Roubini, 'Drastic Action Needed to Avert Global Meltdown', *Australian Financial Review* (24–25 September 2011): 62.

Financial Crisis has exposed how outright corruption had spread through the highest levels of financial and banking services. In mid-2012, the Libor (London inter-bank offer rate) scandal, involving leading banks in the City of London and other global financial centres manipulating interest rates between banks, has hugely damaged their reputation for integrity. The US Commodity Futures Trading Commission listed at least a thousand trillion dollars of potentially affected financial instruments. Potential damages from aggrieved parties could reach hundreds of billions of dollars.[6]

The crisis has struck at the very heart of western financial networks. The chair of Britain's Financial Services Authority and visiting professor at the London School of Economics, Lord Adair Turner, claimed that misconduct by Barclays revealed 'a degree of cynicism and greed which is really quite shocking' and suggests that deep cultural issues need to be addressed. Corruption appears deep-seated. The largest financial institution in Europe, HSBC, has been found laundering money for drug cartels in Mexico and failing to control money transfers to North Korea, Cuba and Sudan. 'HSBC and its affiliates failed to monitor $US60 trillion in wire transfer and account activity.'[7]

US Vice President Dick Cheney claimed that nobody saw the crisis coming, but many did. In an address to the International Monetary Fund in Washington DC in September 2006 Roubini predicted that a looming housing bust could result in a crisis affecting finance and banking, leading to a deep recession.[8] His *Crisis Economics* attacked the 'free market fundamentalism', the perverse incentives of huge bonuses in financial sectors, the failure of regulators and the corruption of the ratings agencies.[9]

As far back as 1991, Robert Kuttner in *The End of Laissez-Faire* had warned against a utopian version of capitalism that relied too exclusively on maximising profits to the exclusion of wider social goals.[10] He argued that markets were needed but limited in scope,

---

6. 'Libor Scandal Goes Global', *Australian Financial Review* (14–15 July, 2012): 15.
7. Justin O'Brien, 'Where the Buck Stops', *Australian Financial Review* (27 July 2012), Review, 10.
8. O'Brien, 'Where the Buck Stops', 1–2.
9. O'Brien, 'Where the Buck Stops', 32–33.
10. Robert Kuttner, *The End of Laissez-Faire: National Purpose and the Global Economy after the Cold War* (New York: University of Pennsylvania Press, 1991),

and tended 'to crowd out other values'.¹¹ He had elsewhere indicted the 'grotesque extremes of wealth and poverty' that resulted from laissez-faire ideology. 'The oldest chestnut in the conservative mythology is the claim that… if we truly wish to help the poor, the best strategy is to stop hobbling the rich, for they are the source of society's wealth and growth.'¹²

In similar vein, Richard C Leone wrote that 'Democrats and moderate Republicans are falling all over each other to prove their conversion to the one true faith of laissez-faire economics'. Leone criticised the 'near religious adherence to the faith' in privatisation, deregulation, downsizing, shrinking entitlements and lower taxes, and the contention that 'virtually all public-sector activity, including financial support for the poor, protection of labor-union rights, and even macroeconomic policies, does more harm than good'.¹³

Paul Krugman in 2009 castigated the blindness of the economics profession 'to the very possibility of catastrophic failures in a market economy'. He singled out the Chicago School of economics for its 'intellectual collapse' and as a 'product of the Dark Age of macroeconomics'.¹⁴ Forgetting the lessons of the Great Depression, 'economists fell back in love with the old, idealised vision of an economy in which rational individuals interact in perfect markets, this time gussied up with fancy equations.'

They turned a blind eye to the limitations of human rationality that often lead to bubbles and busts; to the problem of institutions that run amok; to the imperfections of markets—especially financial markets—that can cause the economy's operating system to undergo sudden unpredictable crashes; and to the dangers created when regulators don't believe in regulation.

He traced the key failure to the belief in neoclassical economics that 'we should have faith in the market system'.¹⁵

5.
11. Kuttner, *The End of Laissez-Faire*, 263.
12. Kuttner, *The End of Laissez-Faire*, 286–87.
13. Richard C Leone, 'Foreword' in Robert Kuttner, *Everything for Sale: The Virtues and Limits of Markets* (Chicago: University of Chicago Press, 1999), x–xi.
14. Paul Krugman, 'Rethinking Economics', *Australian Financial Review*, (11 September 2009): Review, 1. Reprinted from *New York Times Magazine*, 6 September 2009.
15. Paul Krugman, 'Rethinking Economics', 1.

The Promotion of Neoliberal Ideology

The dominant form of neoliberal ideology arose within neoclassical economics but developed as a reaction to Keynesian economics and became aligned with the sectional interests of major international companies. This did not happen by chance. It was the result of determined efforts by major corporations and wealthy interests to advance their commercial interests.

Sharon Beder in his 2006 book, *Free Market Missionaries: the Corporate Manipulation of Community Values,* wrote that this 'free market gospel' suited certain interests. 'The ideology of the "free market" derives from neoclassical economics, but it is a simplified and reduced version that actually distorts and exaggerates neoclassical economic theories.'[16] Friedrich Hayek, Ludwig von Mises and Milton Friedman founded the Mont Pèlerin Society (named after a mountain in Switzerland near where they met) in 1947, which gained influence in the early 1970s and helped develop in a network of institutions, think tanks, governments and corporations around the world.

In his 1967 book, *Capitalism and Freedom,* Friedman denied that corporate officials and stockholders had any obligations other than serving the interests of their stockholders and their members: 'there is one and only one social responsibility of business–to use its resources and engage in activities designed to increase its profits, so long as it stays within the rules of the game, which is to say engages in open and free competition, without deception or fraud.'

> Few trends could so thoroughly undermine the very foundations of our free society as the acceptance by corporate officials of a social responsibility other than to make as much money for their stockholders as possible. This is a fundamentally subversive doctrine.[17]

The ideas promoted in this network were variously named 'neoliberalism in Europe, neo-conservatism, in the US, and

---

16. Sharon Beder, *Free Market Missionaries: The Corporate Manipulation of Community Values* (London: Earthscan, 2006), 6.
17. Milton Friedman, *Capitalism and Freedom* (Chicago: University of Chicago Press, 1967), 133.

economic rationalism or economic fundamentalism in Australia', and aimed at privatisation of government services, deregulation of labour and financial markets, free trade, and smaller government through reduced taxes, spending and regulation.[18]

These conservative groups and organisations became particularly influential during the Reagan and Thatcher periods. Generously funded by wealthy interests, they developed sophisticated campaigns to reshape public opinion in support of their goals. By 1985, the American Enterprise Institute employed 176 people, with ninety adjunct scholars and a budget of $12.6 million, forty-five per cent of which came from 600 major corporations. The AEI employed ghost writers on behalf of scholars to prepare op-ed articles for a hundred newspapers at a rate of three articles every two weeks, produced a monthly TV show screened on over 400 television stations, and a weekly talk program over 180 radio stations.[19] George W Bush admitted that about '150 of his administration came from the Heritage Foundation, the Hoover Institute and the AEI alone.'[20] Beder wrote that during the 1990s, 'more than 80 think tanks employed about 1600 people and each year published about 9000 reports and discussion papers and held 600 conferences and symposia.'[21]

The Business Roundtable, founded in the USA in 1972, spent close to $900 million a year to promote these neoliberal ideas through think tanks like the American Enterprise Institute and the Heritage Foundation.[22]

Similar groups developed in Australia, including the Centre for Independent Studies in 1976 in Sydney, the Institute of Public Affairs, and the HR Nicholls Society, set up in 1986 'to attack union power and the arbitration system and advocate a deregulated labour market'.[23]

However, Professor Ross Garnaut commented in *The Great Crash of 2008* that Australia was saved from some of the excesses of neoliberal ideology:

---

18. Beder, *Free Market Missionaries*, 95.
19. Beder, *Free Market Missionaries*, 117.
20. Beder, *Free Market Missionaries*, 121.
21. Beder, *Free Market Missionaries*, 136.
22. David Harvey, *A Brief History of Neoliberalism* (Oxford: Oxford University Press, 2005/07), 43–44.
23. Beder, *Free Market Missionaries* 127, 135.

> Extreme versions of libertarian economic thought were hardly represented in relevant Australian intellectual life, and not at all in government or the regulatory agencies . . . Australian policy making was generally more autonomous of business money than the American model. Although there was some movement of senior staff between banks and regulators, [in Australia] it was mainly from the public into the private sector.[24]

However, sub-prime loans were also expanding in Australia, especially in western Sydney, rising to about 1 per cent of the mortgage market, amounting to hundreds of millions of dollars. 'Companies like Allco were just starting to push Australia towards the crazy lending practices' of the USA.[25]

The neoliberal ideology took hold in global markets as well as in the UK and US governments, along with a more extreme 'libertarian' view 'that individuals can be left to pursue their own interests independently of social constraints. This view is associated with the writings of Ayn Rand, among others. The major figure in public policy who acknowledged the strong influence of such views was Alan Greenspan.'[26]

After the financial crisis, Greenspan, chairman of the Federal Reserve from 1987 to 2006, confessed to the US Congress the failure of the ideas behind the free market experiment. 'The whole intellectual edifice collapsed . . . I made a mistake in presuming that the self-interests of organizations, specifically banks and others, were such as that they were best capable of protecting their own shareholders and their equity in the firms . . . I was shocked.'[27] He should not have been.

As the well-known financier and philanthropist, George Soros, wrote, markets 'are not capable, on their own, of taking care of collective needs. Nor are they competent to ensure social justice.

---

24. Ross Garnaut, *The Great Crash of 2008* (Melbourne: Melbourne University Publishing, 2009), 142.
25. Geoff Winestock, 'Australia's Very Own Sub-prime Mess', *Australian Financial Review* (27-28 September 2008), 22.
26. Garnaut, *The Great Crash of 2008*, 222.
27. Nicholas Wapshott, *Keynes Hayek: The Clash that Defined Modern Economics* (Melbourne: Scribe, 2011), 279.

These "public goods" can only be provided by a political process.' He added that the shift of the burden of taxation from the rich to the poor and middle classes was no accident, but 'was exactly what the market fundamentalists intended.'[28]

This neoliberal economic ideology has been strongly contested in Australia for decades. Michael Pusey in the early 1990s argued that some contemporary economists had a very ideological view of economic policies, lacking an adequate ethical framework with which to evaluate their ideas.[29] Alan Kohler warned against economics becoming the 'main focus of society' and suffering as a discipline as a result, instead becoming 'one of the principal chariots of dogma in our society'.[30] Kenneth Davidson wrote that in a 'secular, market-driven society, economists have become priests.'[31] The real task of the economic rationalist 'is to convince the rich that their greed is the engine whose generation creates wealth for the whole community'.[32]

John Quiggin in 2012 summed up the results neatly: 'All the evidence supports the commonsense conclusion that policies designed to benefit the rich at the expense of the poor have done precisely that.'[33]

Economics and Morality

Despite this push by neoliberal and neoconservative groups, other economists were aware of the weaknesses at the moral core of much economics. Some of the most prominent of these were Amartya Sen, who has done detailed analysis of the philosophy of economics; Joseph Stiglitz, a prominent critic of neoliberal economics, and who

---

28. George Soros, *The Bubble of American Supremacy* (Sydney: Allen & Unwin, 2004), 91–92.
29. Michael Pusey, *The Experience of Middle Australia: The Dark Side of Economic Reform*, (Cambridge: Cambridge University Press, 2003), 7 ff. For a more extensive Australian critique, see John Wright, *The Ethics of Economic Rationalism* (Sydney: University of New South Wales Press, 1993).
30. Alan Kohler, 'Economics or Dogma', in *The Trouble with Economic Rationalism*, edited by Donald Horne (Melbourne: Scribe, 1992), 100.
31. Kenneth Davidson, 'Do Economists Understand Us?', in *The Trouble with Economic Rationalism*, 60.
32. Davidson, 'Do Economists Understand Us?', 62.
33. John Quiggin, *Zombie Economics: How Dead Ideas Still Walk Among Us* (Melbourne: Black Inc., 2012), 155.

speaks out of extensive experience; and Jeffrey Sachs, one of the architects of the UN Millennium Development Goals.

Amartya Sen
Decades ago in *On Ethics and Economics* Amartya Sen criticised neoclassical economics for characterising 'human motivation in such spectacularly narrow terms', excluding more fundamental questions about how we are to live. He argued against the assumptions that self-interest maximisation best approximated actual human behaviour and that it led to the best economic outcome. Sen recalled that the father of modern economics, Adam Smith, professor of moral philosopher at the University of Glasgow, taught economics as a branch of ethics.[34] The ethics-related approach was derived of course from Aristotle, who considered the making of money as subordinate to the good for the human being and the State.[35]

However, it is what Sen calls the 'engineering approach' which dominated modern economics, impoverishing the discipline by its neglect of normative analysis and of ethical considerations in human behaviour.[36] Sen argued that 'universal selfishness as a requirement of rationality is patently absurd.'[37]

Sen continued that the neoclassical framework eschewed ethical considerations, looking at economic outcomes in terms of 'economic efficiency', though this was quite consistent with extreme inequality.[38] Underlying this view of economics was a utilitarian philosophy which ranked matters according to utility as the only source of value[39] and employed a consequentialist logic, evaluating the goodness of action by outcomes.[40]

Joseph Stiglitz
Another prominent critic of the free market ideology is Joseph Stiglitz, one of the world's leading economists, a member from 1993 and later chair of the Council of Economic Advisers to President

---

34. Amartya Sen, *On Ethics and Economics* (Oxford: Blackwell, 1987/92), 2.
35. Sen, *On Ethics and Economics*, 3–4.
36. Sen, *On Ethics and Economics*, 7.
37. Sen, *On Ethics and Economics*, 16.
38. Sen, *On Ethics and Economics*, 32.
39. Sen, *On Ethics and Economics*, 47.
40. Sen, *On Ethics and Economics*, 39.

Bill Clinton, and Senior Vice-President and Chief Economist at the World Bank from 1997 to 2000. He was awarded the Nobel Prize in 2001 for demonstrating how lack of perfect information undermined the theory of free market efficiency.[41] Later professor at Columbia University, he is a member of the Pontifical Academy for Social Sciences.

He said in interview in 2009: 'Greed does not fully describe the outrageous behaviour of our bankers. What they did was prey on the poorest Americans—it was greed without any moral conscience.' He also blamed the financial system so constructed that no one was accountable for the moral consequences. He considered the US government bailout of US banks as a 'moral outrage',[42] for bailing out those who had caused the crisis while doing little to aid those losing their homes and jobs.

In a series of important books, Stiglitz had earlier attacked the International Monetary Fund for its policies, which 'seemed a curious blend of ideology and bad economics, dogma that sometimes seemed to be thinly veiling special interests'.[43] Choosing his words carefully, he wrote: 'You won't find hard evidence of a terrible conspiracy by Wall Street and the IMF to take over the world. I don't believe such a conspiracy exists. The truth is subtler.'[44]

In his view, the international institutions were dominated by the 'commercial and financial interests' of wealthy countries.[45] Writing soon after the East Asian financial crisis, he said the IMF had encouraged the 'excessively rapid financial and capital market liberalization',[46] and then after the rapid exit of foreign capital forced governments to repay debts and cut services as well as fuel and food subsidies, bankrupting businesses and prompting food riots. 'For

---

41. Gerald Houseman, *Economics in a Changed Universe: Joseph Stiglitz, Globalization and the Death of 'Free Enterprise'* (Lanham MD: Lexington, 2009), 2.
42. Edward Pentin, 'Human rights in jeopardy: bankers' blunders', 7 May 2009, Zenit, at www.zenit.org/article-25809?1=english
43. Joseph E Stiglitz, *Globalization and its Discontents* (London: Allen Lane, 2002), xiii.
44. Stiglitz, *Globalization and its Discontents*, xv.
45. Stiglitz, *Globalization and its Discontents*, 18.
46. Stiglitz, *Globalization and its Discontents*, 89.

many, [globalisation] seems close to an unmitigated disaster."[47]

In his 2006 book, *Making Globalization Work: The Next Step to Global Justice*, Stiglitz advanced an agenda to increase economic development on a more equitable basis. He reiterated his critique of 'market fundamentalism' and the dominance of corporate and financial interests at the expense of poorer countries.[48] He rejected the narrow version of the 'Washington Consensus', with its advocacy of smaller government, deregulation of markets, rapid liberalisation of trade and finance, and privatisation of government assets and businesses, while neglecting issues of equity and employment.[49] He also attacked the negotiations on international trade that overwhelmingly benefited richer countries and hurt poorer ones.[50] 'Special interests are largely to blame... in the developed world shaping the agenda to benefit themselves'.[51] He was especially concerned about the influence of the major corporations (pharmaceuticals, Microsoft, ExxonMobil and agricultural interests) corrupting the political process through their donations to both political parties.[52]

> For much of the world, globalization as it has been managed seems like a pact with the devil . . . closer integration into the global economy has brought greater volatility and insecurity, and more inequality. It has even threatened fundamental values.[53]

Continuing his critique in 2010 in *Freefall: America, Free Markets, and the Sinking of the World Economy*, Stiglitz charged that the Great Recession had destroyed faith in the doctrines about the efficiency of free markets, and the belief in small government and minimal regulation.[54] Not only was the philosophy behind neoliberalism

---

47. *Ibid.*, 20.
48. Joseph E Stiglitz, *Making Globalization Work: the Next Step to Global Justice* (London: Alan Lane, 2006), 10.
49. Stiglitz, *Making Globalization Work*, 17,
50. Stiglitz, *Making Globalization Work*, 62 ff.
51. Stiglitz, *Making Globalization Work*, 79.
52. Stiglitz, *Making Globalization Work*, 278.
53. Stiglitz, *Making Globalization Work*, 292.
54. Joseph E Stiglitz, *Freefall: America, Free Markets, and the Sinking of the World Economy* (New York: WW Norton, 2010), xi–xii.

at fault, but he castigated the economics profession itself which provided the rhetoric for special interest groups exploiting an economic ideology. He wrote that 'all the critical policies, such as those related to deregulation, were the consequence of political and economic "forces"—interests, ideas and ideologies—that go beyond individuals . . . The problem was not so much Greenspan as the deregulatory ideology that had taken hold.'[55]

> That those policies had been shaped by special interests—of the financial markets—is obvious. More complex is the role of economics. Among the long list of those to blame for the crisis, I would include the economics profession, for it provided the special interests with arguments about efficient and self-regulating markets—even though advances in economics during the preceding two decades had shown the limited conditions under which that theory held true.[56]

At World Economic Forum meetings Stiglitz had regularly predicted an approaching crisis, though by 2007 the global growth rate reached seven per cent.[57] 'The only surprise about the economic crisis of 2008 was that it came as a surprise to so many. For a few observers, it was a textbook case that was not only predicable but also predicted.'[58] In response to claims that the crisis was unforeseeable, Stiglitz charged that 'too much money was being made by too many people for their warnings to be heard'. As well as himself expecting the US economy to crash, with international consequences, he instanced Nouriel Roubini, George Soros, Stephen Roach, Robert Shiller and Robert Wescott also doing so.[59]

---

55. Stiglitz, *Freefall*, xvii.
56. Stiglitz, *Freefall*, xx-xxi.
57. Stiglitz, *Freefall:*, xxi.
58. Stiglitz, *Freefall:*, 1.
59. Stiglitz, *Freefall*, 18. In Australia, the mathematical economists, Steve Keen and the late Wynne Godley also warned of the approaching crisis. See Steve Keen, 'The Future of Economics', *OnLine Opinion*, 1 February 2012 www.onlineopinion.com.au/print.asp?article+13191 .

This 'near-death experience' of the global economy 'exposed not only flaws in the prevailing economic model but also flaws in our society.'[60]

> We have gone far down an alternative path—creating a society in which materialism dominates moral commitment, in which the rapid growth that we have achieved is not sustainable environmentally or socially, in which we do not act together as a community to address our common needs, partly because rugged individualism and market fundamentalism have eroded any sense of community . . . [61]

He continued that 'too little has been written about the underlying "moral deficit" that has been exposed [by the] unrelenting pursuit of profits and the elevation of the pursuit of self-interest'.[62]

In *The Stiglitz Report: Reforming the International Monetary and Financial Systems in the Wake of the Global Financial Crisis*, written at the request of the President of the UN General Assembly, Miguel D'Escoto Brockman, to advise the June 2010 Summit on the financial crisis, Stiglitz reiterated that 'the regulatory regime may have been affected more by the influence of certain special interests than the merits of theoretical arguments'.[63] He warned that these powerful interests could reinforce their control and inequity, but he hoped for major changes promoting 'social justice and social solidarity', especially for the developing countries and the environment.[64]

Stiglitz developed his proposals for economic reconstruction in 2012 in *The Price of Inequality: How Today's Divided Society Endangers our Future*. He wrote markets must be tamed so that they benefited most citizens:

---

60. Stiglitz, *Freefall*, 275.
61. Stiglitz, *Freefall*, 275–76.
62. Stiglitz, *Freefall*, 278,
63. Joseph E Stiglitz, *The Stiglitz Report: Reforming the International Monetary and Financial Systems in the Wake of the Global Financial Crisis* (New York: Free Press, 2010), 64.
64. Stiglitz, *The Stiglitz Report*, 198, 195.

> Something has happened to our sense of values, when the end of making more money justifies the means . . . Much of what has gone on can only be described by the words 'moral deprivation'. Something wrong happened to the moral compass of so many of the people working in the financial sector and elsewhere. [65]

He concluded: 'While globalization may benefit society as a whole, it has left many behind—not a surprise given that, to a large extent, globalization has been managed by corporate and other special interests for their benefit.'[66]

Jeffrey Sachs
Other leading economists are among those calling for a return to 'civic virtue . . . to reconnect public values and public policy',[67] to rescue capitalism from decay and collapse. The prominent economist and Director of the Earth Institute in Columbia University, Jeffrey Sachs, in *The Price of Civilization*, wrote:

> Wall Street's meltdown in 2007–08 had all the makings of a morality tale, with greedy bankers claiming to be doing 'God's work', corrupt politicians fawning on Wall Street in search of campaign contributions, and a hapless public left to foot the bill for trillions of dollars of newly added public debt.[68]

The United States had 'let market institutions run wild over politics and public values', resulting in extreme inequality and destroying the credibility of governments. The contagion had spread worldwide,

---

65. Joseph Stiglitz, *The Price of Inequality: How Today's Divided Society Endangers our Future* (New York: WW Norton, 2012), xvii.
66. Stiglitz, *The Price of Inequality*, 277.
67. Jeffrey Sachs, *The Price of Civilization: Economics and Ethics after the Fall* (London: The Bodley Head, 2011), x.
68. Sachs, *The Price of Civilization*, ix. The CEO of Goldman Sachs, Lloyd Blankfein, had defended the extraordinary earnings of investment bankers like himself as doing 'God's work'. See Will Hutton, 'The Financial Crisis and the End of the Hunter-Gatherer', in Rowan Williams, *Crisis and Recovery: Ethics, Economics and Justice* (London: Palgrave Macmillan, 2010), 185.

with its 'corruption, corporate power, environmental threats, and psychological destabilization'.[69]

Sachs is caustic in his critique of the deregulated markets, tax cuts for the rich and reduced social spending that has resulted in widening inequality. 'Globalization unleashed vast corporate power and undermined whole regions'.[70] He continued: 'The key question today is global and urgent: how can capitalism in the twenty-first century deliver the three overarching goals sought by societies around the world: economic prosperity, social justice, and environmental sustainability?'[71]

Sachs was 'unnerved to have to write this book'. He had spent much of his professional life addressing problems of the developing countries, and had coordinated the development of the UN Millennium Development Goals campaign. He is dismayed by the financial and economic crises in the United States and Europe. 'At the root of America's economic crisis lies a moral crisis: the decline of civic virtue among America's political and economic elite . . . Without restoring an ethos of social responsibility, there can be no meaningful and sustained economic recovery.'[72] 'Too many of America's elite—among the super-rich, the CEOs, and many of my colleagues in academia—have abandoned a commitment to social responsibility. They chase wealth and power, the rest of society be damned.'[73]

Sachs is especially critical of major corporations opposing action to deal with climate change. 'Big Oil has played a notorious role in the fight to keep climate change off the U.S. agenda. Exxon-Mobil, Koch Industries, and others in the sector have underwritten a generation of antiscientific propaganda to confuse the American people.'[74]

The economic system itself is skewed to increase inequality: 'At the start of the 1970s, average top 100 CEO pay was roughly 40 times the average worker's pay. By the year 2000, it had reached 1,000 times the average worker's pay!' while 'the median take-home pay of male full-time workers (adjusted for inflation) has stagnated since the

---

69. Sachs, *The Price of Civilization*, xi.
70. Sachs, *The Price of Civilization* xii.
71. Sachs, *The Price of Civilization*, xv.
72. Sachs, *The Price of Civilization*, 3.
73. Sachs, *The Price of Civilization*, 45.
74. Sachs, *The Price of Civilization*, 118.

1970s.'[75] 'The wealthiest 1 percent of American households today enjoys a higher total net worth than the bottom 90 percent, and the top 1 percent of income earners receives more pre-tax income than the bottom 50 percent.'[76]

'The corporate income tax is now a sieve, with so many loopholes and ways to shelter income in foreign tax havens that the tax collection has declined from round 3.5 percent of GDP in the 1960s to around 1.5 percent of GDP now.'[77] Sachs points out that even Google uses tax havens like Bermuda to avoid paying billions of dollars in taxes.[78] The result is that '... the income tax rates paid by the richest 1 percent have declined markedly from 1980 till now, falling from around 34.5 percent of income in 1980 to around 23.2 percent of income in 2008.'[79] Like many other large corporations, Apple too reportedly evades billions of dollars a year in tax and via transfers to low-tax countries.[80]

Stiglitz concurs:

> Likewise, part of the wealth of those in finance comes from exploiting the poor, through predatory lending, and abusive credit-card practices. It might not be so bad if there were even a grain of truth to trickle-down economics... But most Americans today are worse off–with lower real (inflation-adjusted) incomes–than they were in 1997.

America 'has become a country not "with justice for all", but rather with favouritism for the rich and justice for those who can afford it'—as was evident in the big banks not being held accountable.[81]

What consistently emerges from many economists is the call for better moral foundations for economic theory and practice. Robert Skidelsky wrote:

---

75. Sachs, *The Price of Civilization*, 20–21.
76. Sachs, *The Price of Civilization*, 22–23.
77. Sachs, *The Price of Civilization*, 231.
78. Sachs, *The Price of Civilization*, 127.
79. Sachs, *The Price of Civilization*, 234–35.
80. Charles Duhigg and David Kocieniewski, 'Letterbox in Luxembourg one way Apple avoids paying billions in worldwide tax', *The Age* (30 April 2012).
81. Stiglitz, 'Trickle-up Wealth is Making the American Dream a Myth', *The Age* (9 June 2012).

> At the heart of the moral failure is the worship of growth for its own sake, rather than as a way to achieve the 'good life'. As a result, economic efficiency—the means to growth—has been given absolute priority in our thinking and policy. The only moral compass we now have is the thin and degraded notion of economic welfare. This moral lacuna explains uncritical acceptance of globalization and financial innovation.[82]

Former Australian Liberal leader, John Hewson, wrote: 'I quite frankly despair at times at how these "value issues" are so easily ignored' in public debate. He argued that we need to look at policy issues 'from the point of view of the sort of society we want to live in.'[83]

Restoring the 'Good Society'

Sachs argues that America needs to recover 'the idea of a good society', with people paying their fair share of taxes, being alert to the needs of others, acting as stewards for future generations, and 'remembering that compassion is the glue that holds a society together'.[84]

> Our greatest national illusion is that a healthy society can be organized around the single-minded pursuit of wealth. The ferocity of the quest for wealth throughout society has left Americans exhausted and deprived of the benefits of social trust, honesty, and compassion. Our society has turned harsh, with the elites on Wall Street, in Big Oil, and in Washington among the most irresponsible and selfish of all.[85]

Instead, he calls for a return to a society that 'promotes the personal virtues of self-awareness and moderation, and the civic virtues of compassion' and cooperation across class, ethnic or religious divides.[86]

---

82. Robert Skidelsky, 'Keynes mark II', *Australian Financial Review* (13 February 2009): Review 3.
83. John Hewson, 'Moral leadership lacking', *Australian Financial Review,* (24 April 2009).
84. Sachs, *Price of Civilization*, 5.
85. Sachs, *Price of Civilization,* 9.
86. Sachs, *Price of Civilization*, 10.

Even Mikhail Gorbachev called for new moral foundations for economies, rejecting the 'pernicious and immoral pyramid' of laissez-faire economics, which was so 'destructive and often corrupt'.[87]

Likewise Tomas Sedlacek in *Economics of Good and Evil* argues for a reordering of public values to focus on pursuit of the genuine good for human beings. He insists that the fundamental questions that economists often try to ignore relate to questions of meaning, of good and evil, and of what Schumacher called in *Small is Beautiful*, 'meta-economics', and the values hidden below economic thinking.[88] Sedlacek writes that modern economics needs to recover an historical perspective on the development of human understanding about values and what is the good to be sought in life.[89]

He highlights the neglect of ethics. 'The issue of good and evil was dominant in classical debates, yet today it is almost heretical to even talk about it.' Though Adam Smith extolled sympathy for others as basic in social life, later economic thinkers seized on Smith's metaphor of the 'invisible hand' and transformed it into a belief that moral decisions could be left to the market.[90] 'Smith's legacy is that moral questions must be included in economics—that is the key question of economics.'[91]

Robert Shiller in *Finance and the Good Society* contends that the financial crisis 'was not due simply to the greed or dishonesty of players in the world of finance; it was ultimately due to fundamental structural shortcomings in our financial institutions' which were still not addressed.[92] He called for 'redistributions through a progressive income tax . . . without raising alarms that wealth might be unfairly confiscated.'[93]

Shiller rejects the view that 'the subprime mortgage collapse that brought on the current financial crisis was a deliberate plot by Countrywide and other mortgage lenders', or that they acted

---

87. Mikhail Gorbachev, 'Mr Capitalism, Tear down that Immorality', *Australian Financial Review* (31 October 2008): 65.
88. Tomas Sedlacek, *Economics of Good and Evil: The Quest for Economic Meaning from Gilgamesh to Wall Street* (Oxford: Oxford University Press, 2011), 7.
89. Sedlacek, *Economics of Good and Evil*, 9.
90. Sedlacek, *Economics of Good and Evil*, 198.
91. Sedlacek, *Economics of Good and Evil*, 210.
92. Robert J Shiller, *Finance and the Good Society* (Princeton NJ: Princetown University Press, 2012), xii.
93. Shiller, *Finance and the Good Society*, 235.

'deliberately in full knowledge of the actual outcome'.[94] In other words, it resulted from stupidity, ideology and greed, not from a deliberate conspiracy to undermine the economy.

As is apparent from these comments, there is widespread alarm about the power of financial capital and global corporations. In the view of Sachs, the concentration of wealth has resulted in growing inequality and the capture of political and economic power by major corporations. 'The large and growing role of big money in politics is the grim political reality of our times. It is the key to understanding the expanding tentacles of the corporatocracy.'[95]

Stefano Zamagni also sees the concentration of economic power as a threat to democracy: 'a market which deflects democracy from its horizons in order to make room just for efficiency . . . pushes the economy along a path of oligarchic development', forgetting 'that democracy and freedom are values superior to it.'[96]

Role of Christian Values?

The churches have long critiqued the philosophical flaws in much of economics, insisting that the economy must serve human needs and the wellbeing of everyone with reasonable equity, and not concentrate wealth in the hands of an elite. Many writers from Christian traditions have addressed these issues. As Duncan Forrester wrote in 1989 in *Beliefs, Values and Policies*:

> Back in the 1920s R.H. Tawney was already arguing that theology had been driven out of the public arena, or had chosen to evacuate it, leaving in possession not a natural code of decency, prudence, and fair play, but another creed, 'a persuasive, self-confident and militant Gospel proclaiming the absolute value of economic success'... Tawney saw this new gospel – which has in recent years returned with renewed force and arrogance – as a false gospel, a modern paganism fundamentally opposed to the Christian faith and Christian values, and hence a denial of the justice of God, involving oppression of

---

94. Shiller, *Finance and the Good Society*, 220.
95. Sachs, *Price of Civilization*, 109.
96. Stefano Zamagni, 'The proximate and remote Causes of a Crisis foretold: a View from Catholic Social Thought', in *Crisis in a Global Economy*, 316. Zamagni is reportedly one of the main drafters of Pope Benedict's *Caritas in Veritate*.

the poor and weak and the glorification of the rich and powerful.[97]

Forrester quoted Michael Ignatieff that we lack 'a shared language of the good', and that the 'generalised silence' in our secular culture about spiritual needs dodges questions of ultimate meaning.[98] Wealth and moneymaking try to fill the void, often at the expense of the poor.[99]

Yet the churches have had great difficulty engaging constructively with contemporary social thinkers about the moral foundations of economics. Our more cynical and secular culture can dismiss Christian thinking on economics as naïve moralising. And the churches themselves have at times failed to establish credibility in this conversation, even though their charitable and welfare works are abundant.

Problems in the encounter between Christian thinkers and economists also arise because of the disturbing gap between moral philosophy and contemporary economics. Positivism in economics has resulted in a widespread impression that economics with its mathematical precision can give reliable and scientific direction. Wiser economists insist that economics is a *social* science, and that it is a huge error to consider it akin to the physical sciences or mathematics. Economics is enmeshed in the decision-making of human beings, subject to all the whims and unpredictability of which people are capable, as well as that of wider events.

Christian thinkers and activists have certainly been influential in debates about international debt, global development, and peace and disarmament issues. Public campaigns by the churches and other groups mobilised public opinion to support the remission of much of the debt of the most impoverished countries under the HPIC (Heavily Indebted Poor Countries) initiative at the turn of the century. Such activism will presumably increase since most Christians now live in developing countries. Confronted daily by savage poverty and injustice in various parts of the world, many Church leaders and thinkers have been strong critics of how the global economy is geared to favour the rich developed countries.

In response to the Global Financial Crisis, the Anglican Archbishop of Canterbury, Rowan Williams, organised a conference

---

97. Duncan Forrester, *Beliefs, Values and Policies* (Oxford: Clarendon Press, 1989), 46.
98. Forrester, *Beliefs*, 47.
99. Forrester, *Beliefs*, 58.

with leading British thinkers in March 2009 at Lambeth Palace. He wrote:

> The economic ills of the last couple of years have brought to light a widespread anxiety about the kind of society we have become, and even more, the kind of human person... In trivializing the meaning of wealth, we have also reduced the range of human reflection and questioning around wellbeing and the good life.[100]

He pleaded for 'a renewal of political culture and social vision, a renewal of civic energy and creativity'.[101]

> The isolated *homo economicus* of the old textbooks, making rational calculations of self-interest, has been exposed as a straw man: the search for profit at a fantastic cost in terms of risk and unrealism has shown that there can be a form of economic 'rationality' that is in fact wildly irrational.[102]

The most consistent Christian effort to shape economic and social thought can perhaps be found in the papal encyclicals. Pope Leo XIII initiated the modern papal critique of economics in his 1891 encyclical, *Rerum Novarum*.[103] Leo used the terms 'economic liberalism' as a synonym for Manchester or 'laissez-faire' capitalism to typify the versions of capitalism to which he most objected. The term 'economic liberalism' functions in Church documents almost as a Weberian 'type' and can be confusing for English-speaking

---

100. Rowan Williams, 'Foreword', in Rowan Williams and Larry Elliott, *Crisis and Recovery*, xi.
101. Williams, 'Foreword', xiii.
102. Rowan Williams, 'Knowing our Limits', in Williams and Elliott, *Crisis and Recovery*, 24.
103. For recent commentaries on Catholic social thought, see *Compendium of the Social Doctrine of the Church* (Vatican City: Libreria Editrice Vaticana, 2004); John Sniegocki, *Catholic Social Teaching and Economic Globalization: the Quest for Alternatives* (Milwaukee WI: Marquette University Press, 2009); *Modern Catholic Social Teaching: Commentaries and Interpretations*, edited by Kenneth R Himes (Washington DC: Georgetown University Press, 2004); and JS Boswell, FP McHugh and J Verstraeten, *Catholic Social Thought: Twilight or Renaissance?* (Peeters Leuven: Leuven University Press, 2000).

audiences for whom 'liberalism' does not have such heavy ideological and elitist overtones as it had in Europe.

During the Great Depression, Pope Pius XI in 1931 condemned the vast inequalities in wealth and the injustice suffered by the poor, and particularly criticised the Manchester school of economics which allowed wages to fall to subsistence levels. 'But free competition, while justified and certainly useful provided it is kept within certain limits, clearly cannot direct economic life' and must be subject to effective regulation to conform to social justice.[104]

Pope Paul VI in *Development of Peoples* (1967) condemned an 'unchecked liberalism', 'a system which . . . considers profit as the key motive for economic progress, competition as the supreme law of economics, and private ownership of the means of production as an absolute right that has no limits and carries no corresponding social obligation'.[105] He continued: 'Without abolishing the competitive market, it should be kept within the limits which make it just and moral', restoring 'to the participants a certain equality of opportunity'.[106]

In light of the global financial crisis, these words are remarkably prescient, and it is no wonder that Pope Benedict XVI in his 2009 encyclical, *Caritas in Veritate*, urged Catholics to view *Development of Peoples* as the new standard in Catholic social thinking, as was *Rerum Novarum* in the past.[107]

Pope John Paul II

To help prepare for the centenary of *Rerum Novarum*, the Vatican invited some leading economists to a consultation in Rome on 5 November 1990. Included were Kenneth J. Arrow, Partha Dasgupta, Jacques H Dreze, and Amartya Sen. The group considered ethical issues about the role of the market, especially the trade-off between

---

104. Pope Pius XI, *Quadragesimo Anno*, 88, at http://www.vatican.va/holy_father/pius_xi/encyclicals/documents/hf_p-xi_enc_19310515_quadragesimo-anno_en.htmlhttp://xroads.virginia.edu/~ma01/Kidd/thesis/pdf/quadragesimo.pdf.
105. Pope Paul VI, *Development of Peoples* (26 March 1967), 26, at http://www.vatican.va/holy_father/paul_vi/encyclicals/documents/hf_p-vi_enc_26031967_populorum_en.html
106. Pope Paul VI, *Development of Peoples*, 61.
107. Pope Benedict XVI, *Caritas in Veritate* (29 June, 2009), 8, at http://www.vatican.va/holy_father/benedict_xvi/encyclicals/documents/hf_ben-xvi_enc_20090629_caritas-in-veritate_en.html

efficiency and equity, the role of government and the problems of hunger in the world.

Kenneth Arrow was in no doubt that competitive markets may distribute goods very inequitably, and that strong mechanisms of redistribution were needed. In the previous decade, the tendency to reduce taxes on the wealthy in many developed countries 'has shown no obvious gains in efficiency while poverty has increased'. The 'relaxation of moral standards and an over-vivid exaltation of the markets and of the value of greed in the last decade have led to new abuses'. He argued that the market should not be the final arbiter. 'Actions of individuals must be governed by moral considerations of consequences and by legal controls'.[108] He looked to the Church to help rouse the moral commitment and motivation of people to tackle poverty and hunger.

In *Centesimus Annus* Pope John Paul II reiterated the Church's critique of capitalism when it excluded most people from any genuine ownership (#6). He said Leo XIII's attack on 'unbridled capitalism' was still relevant, especially in the Third World. Hence 'it is right to speak of a struggle against an economic system, if the latter is understood as a method of upholding the absolute predominance of capital'. He favoured a 'society of free work, of enterprise and of participation. Such a society is not directed against the market, but demands that the market be appropriately controlled by the forces of society and by the State, so as to guarantee that the basic needs of the whole of society are satisfied' (#35). He warned that after the collapse of communism, 'a radical capitalist ideology could spread', blindly entrusting problems to the free development of market forces (#34).

Some Catholic writers, like Michael Novak and his neoconservative colleagues, have been influenced by Hayek and his admirers. Some of these Catholics work for US think tanks and organisations generously funded by private financial interests. They have been vigorous critics of aspects of Catholic social teaching, particularly concerning social or distributive justice. Such a well-financed critique of official Catholic social teaching by Catholic intellectuals is a new phenomenon for English-speaking Catholics, and has confused some people about what the Church formally holds on capitalism.[109]

---

108. Kenneth Arrow, 'Moral Thinking and Economic Interaction', in *Social and Ethical Aspects of Economics: A Colloquium in the Vatican* (Vatican City: Pontifical Commission Justice and Peace, 1992), 19–21.
109. See John Sniegocki, 'The Social Ethics of Pope John Paul II: a Critique of

John Paul consistently reiterated his critique of capitalism. In Mexico in 1990 he said:

> The events of recent history . . . have been interpreted, sometimes superficially, as the triumph of the liberal capitalist system. Particular interests would like to carry the analysis to the extreme of presenting the system they regard as the winner as the only path for our world on the basis of the experience of the setbacks suffered by contemporary socialism, and shunning the critical judgment required toward the effects liberal capitalism has produced in the countries of the so-called Third World.[110]

In Latvia in 1993, John Pope bluntly declared that Catholic social doctrine is not 'a surrogate for capitalism', and that the Church had 'always distanced itself from capitalist ideology, holding it responsible for grave social injustices . . . I myself, after the historical failure of communism, did not hesitate to raise serious doubts on the validity of capitalism.'[111]

In Cuba in January 1998 he again attacked 'a certain capitalist neoliberalism that subordinates the human person to blind market forces . . . From its centres of power, such neoliberalism often places unbearable burdens on less favoured countries . . . In the international community, we thus see a small number of countries growing exceedingly rich at the cost of the increasing impoverishment of a great number of other countries.'[112]

In his 1999 apostolic letter, *Ecclesia in America,* John Paul repeated his critique of the negative dimensions of 'neoliberal' capitalism, with its overemphasis on profit and the free market to the detriment of growing numbers of poor victimised by unjust policies and structures.[113]

Neoconservative Interpretations', in *Horizons,* 33/1 (2006): 7–32.
110. John Paul II, 'Is Liberal Capitalism the only Path?', in *Origins* 20 (24 May 1990): 19.
111. John Paul II, 'What Catholic Social Teaching is and is not', in *Origins,* 23/15 (23 September 1993): 257.
112. John Paul II in a homily of 25 January 1998, quoted in Sniegocki, *Catholic Social Teaching and Economic Globalization,* 148.
113. John Paul II, *Ecclesia in America* (22 January 1999), 56, at http://www.

Speaking to the Pontifical Academy of Social Sciences in April 2001, John Paul noted that 'the market economy seems to have conquered virtually the entire world', but it needed a renewed ethical framework to 'promote a globalization which will be at the service of the whole person and of all people'.[114]

In 2003 he lamented that the 'ideology of the market' resulting 'from a civilization of consumption' tended to reduce people to consumers, making 'solidarity difficult at best', especially for the poor and marginalised.[115]

Closely linked in the thinking of John Paul about economic issues was the need to face threats to the environment. In many documents, he highlighted the moral responsibility of the current generation. In his 1990 World Day of Peace Statement, *The Ecological Crisis: a Common Responsibility*, he warned of the rapid deterioration in the environment and urged action to overcome the 'dangerous' and alarming inertia about the 'crisis', which was also a 'moral crisis'.[116] He called for an 'ecological conversion' to avoid 'catastrophe'. Human beings must exercise their responsibility for the creation as stewards and not as autonomous despots; we 'must stop at the edge of the abyss'.[117] Often he called for more modest lifestyles to avoid the excessive consumption and waste of consumerism, and to ensure that resources were more justly shared.

Pope John Paul II vigorously promoted efforts to reform economic systems and build a more equitable and just world, but as he grew weaker, his social initiatives waned. Pope Benedict XVI has not been able to regain John Paul's momentum on social issues, despite his

---

vatican.va/holy_father/john_paul_ii/apost_exhortations/documents/hf_jp-ii_exh_22011999_ecclesia-in-america_en.html

114. John Paul, Address to the Pontifical Academy of Social Sciences, 27 April 2001, at http://www.vatican.va/holy_father/john_paul_ii/speeches/2001/documents/hf_jp-ii_spe_20010427_pc-social-sciences_en.html
115. John Paul II, Address to new Czech ambassador to the Vatican, 29 April 2003, at http://www.zenit.org/article-7127?l=english .
116. John Paul II, *The Ecological Crisis: A Common Responsibility*, World Day of Peace Statement, 1 January 1990. http://conservation.catholic.org/ecologicalcrisis.htm
117. John Paul II, General audience, 17 January 2001, at http://www.vatican.va/holy_father/john_paul_ii/audiences/2001/documents/hf_jp-ii_aud_20010117_en.html

valuable but ponderous 2009 social encyclical, *Caritas in Veritate*. And few other church leaders have the expertise to take part in debates about these global social and economic issues. Inexplicably, moreover, despite their own social teaching, some of the largest churches fail to put resources into educating their adherents about the moral dimensions of economic issues, and supporting efforts to engage in the public conversation in a serious and sustained way.

Conclusion

In his assessment of the economic crisis, Lord Adair Turner, argued that economics as a discipline needed to be reconstructed. He criticised the dangerous 'perversion and simplification of economics' that had such influence on decision-makers in government and finance.[118] He wanted to see economics more closely connected with political economy, 'a philosophical, empirical, historical and ethical discipline, as well as a rigorously mathematical one'.[119]

He strongly agreed with Keynes that 'economics is a moral and not a natural science', and must be attentive to human nature and institutions. Turner wanted economics to be more aware of how things operate in the real world and the limitations of economic abstractions based on a 'rational' *homo economicus*; people had goals and values beyond economics, notably happiness and wellbeing.[120]

These perceptions about the need for a thorough rethinking about morality and economics are widely shared in the community as well as the economics profession. They are also a plea for renewed commitment to social equity, participation and solidarity in pursuit of human wellbeing for all people in our globalising world.

In Cardinal Turkson's view, four major areas need urgent attention:

(1) the excessive concentration of power;
(2) the inequality between countries;
(3) the distribution of economic resources which conflicts with the wider requirements of the universal destination of earthly goods; and
(4) the use of resources by those who control them

---

118. Adair Turner, *Economics after the Crisis: Objectives and Means* (Cambridge MA: MIT Press, 2012), 91.
119. Turner, *Economics after the Crisis*, xi.
120. Turner, *Economics after the Crisis*, 93–94.

which does not take sufficient account of the need for social justice.[121]

These aspirations for the international economy are undoubtedly very important. But they presuppose commitment to values based on the dignity of the person and the fact that we are all in this together. As Pope Benedict XVI summarised in 2010:

> The worldwide financial breakdown . . . has also shown the error of the assumption that the market is capable of regulating itself, apart from public intervention and the support of internationalized moral standards. This assumption is based on an impoverished notion of economic life as a sort of self-calibrating mechanism driven by self-interest and profit-seeking. As such, it overlooks the essentially ethical nature of economics as an activity *of* and *for* human beings. Rather than a spiral of production and consumption in view of narrowly-defined human needs, economic life should properly be seen as an exercise of human responsibility, intrinsically oriented towards the promotion of the dignity of the person, the pursuit of the common good and the integral development—political,cultural and spiritual—of individuals, families and societies.[122]

Rowan Williams lucidly put it: 'We urgently need to dust off this language of virtue . . . rescuing the concept of civic virtue and connecting it with individual moral wellbeing'.[123] 'So the question of how we think about shared wellbeing is the central one before us.'[124]

---

121. Turkson, 'The Social Doctrine of Benedict XVI in Caritas in Veritate', 53. See also Pontifical Council for Justice and Peace, *Vocation of the Business Leader: a Reflection*, Vatican City: March 2012), at http://www.pcgp.it/dati/2012-05/04-999999/Vocation%20ENG2.pdf .
    Also, *Towards Reforming the International Financial and Monetary Systems in the Context of Global Public Authority* (Vatican City: 24 October 2011), at http://www.vatican.va/roman_curia/pontifical_councils/justpeace/documents/rc_pc_justpeace_doc_20111024_nota_en.html
122. Pope Benedict XVI, Address to Participants in the 16th Plenary Session of the Pontifical Academy, 30 April 2010, in *Crisis in a Global Economy*, 14.
123. Williams, 'Knowing our Limits', 30.
124. Williams, 'Knowing our Limits', 24.

This is surely the core business of the churches among others, instilling and fostering practice of the virtues that constitute authentic human fulfilment, especially of the more disadvantaged. The churches have a splendid record in works of charity and social services, but at times have difficulty seeing how concern for wider issues of social justice also springs from the very heart of Christian belief. This must change. The churches urgently need to put resources into highlighting the link between faith and social justice, not just in their education programs but also with church spokespeople and organisations taking a stronger role in the public forum.

Secondly, local Christian communities must become more involved with social debates. With Catholics in mind, Kenneth Himes warned that it is an error to keep focused on papal statements rather than on the analysis and writing in local and regional churches.[125]

It is not just a matter of renewing social ethics and philosophy. The political implications are daunting, since special interests and the 'corporatocracy' will presumably fight hard to maintain their positions of power and influence.

Fortunately, all those inspired by the Bible can find dramatic imperatives to act justly, but what this means in our changing context needs continually to be refined and clarified. Moreover, economic issues form a key part of the new conversation with other religious and philosophical traditions about the nature of the good and the pursuit of human wellbeing. While there are differences in how we see these at times, there is much we can agree on, as the program of the Millennium Development Goals demonstrates.

The Global Financial Crisis, terrible as it is, offers the world an opportunity to review not just our economic systems but also the values undergirding our societies and civilisation. Without renewed commitment to authentic human values, we are unlikely to secure a sustainable and prosperous future for coming generations.

---

125. Kenneth Himes, 'Globalization with the Human Face: Catholic Social Teaching and Globalization', in *Theological Studies*, 69/2 (June 2008): 288.

The Globalisation of Theology

John D'Arcy May

In 1981 Wilfred Cantwell Smith, the great historian and theologian of understanding among religions, published his Cadbury Lectures under the title: *Towards a World Theology*.[1] This was not the only such venture to have appeared around that time,[2] but its humane person-centred approach to interreligious relations makes it stand out, even today, though it was contested at the time.[3] For Smith, such a global theology was feasible only if suitably informed representatives of religious traditions learned to do theology collaboratively, and he even gave an informal and amusing sketch of how such collaboration might work.[4] As someone whose project was to write a history of religion 'in the singular', however, he was only too well aware of how humanly difficult and methodologically complicated such collaboration would be. For him, each identifiable 'religion'—a word whose use he tried to discourage in the sense of distinct, self-

---

1. WC Smith, *Towards a World Theology: Faith and the Comparative History of Religion* (London: Macmillan, 1981).
2. See, for example, Leonard Swidler, *After the Absolute: The Dialogical Future of Religion* (Minneapolis: Fortress Press, 1990); *Toward a Universal Theology of Religion*, edited by Leonard Swidler (Maryknoll: Orbis Books, 1987); N Ross Reat and E Perry, *A World Theology: The Central Spiritual Reality of Humankind* (Cambridge: Cambridge University Press, 1991).
3. See the rejoinder which Cantwell Smith felt constrained to add to John Hick's concluding remarks after a conference on religious pluralism in which Smith dissented from the abstract *a priori* pluralism of some colleagues, in *Truth and Dialogue: The Relationship Between World Religions*, edited by John Hick (London: Sheldon Press, 1974), 156–162.
4. Smith, *World Theology*, chapter 7.

contained religious entities[5]—was a 'cumulative tradition' which could only be understood (by the historian) through its interactions with other traditions and (by the theologian) by getting some sense of the 'faith' that inspired it, an anthropological constant which it would be found to share with all who were genuinely religious. It is at this point that Smith's programme becomes problematic, but the world theology he envisaged and the conditions he set for achieving it have a new relevance now that the multi-polar, multi-religious shape of the world has been captured by the term 'globalisation'.

I propose to use the term globalisation as a purely formal concept, prompting the question: 'Globalisation of what?' I think it is best understood as the universalising of communication to the point where time and space are compressed to become a continuous present in what Manuel Castells has called the 'real virtuality' created by electronic media[6] (hence expressions such as 'real time' banking, gaming, reporting *etcetera*). On this premise, it makes just as much sense to speak about the globalisation of crime, or benevolence, or security, or trade, as it does to talk about the globalisation of theology. Seen in this light, globalisation is a revolution on a par with the invention of the printing press, but it is also a crisis of information overload, as was evidenced in the global financial crisis of 2008–2009, when financial 'experts' lost control of the enormously complex transactions they were engaging in. Humans are not equipped, either biologically or socially, to cope with such a rapid extension of our sensory apparatus, and its consequences for the ways we imagine, learn, dream, use language and otherwise respond to the world as yet to be fully understood. But in the case of theology the effects of globalisation are particularly far-reaching. Engagement with philosophical movements such as deconstruction and the acknowledgement of post-modernity as a new intellectual context are only the beginnings of our accommodation to religious globalisation.

For me the key question is the emergence of something like a global civil society and the place of the religions in it. Religious traditions are

---

5. WC Smith, *The Meaning and End of Religion* (New York: Macmillan, 1962).
6. Manuel Castells, *The Rise of the Network Society. The Information Age: Economy, Society and Culture,* volume 1 (Oxford: Blackwell, 1996), chapter 6, especially 410–418.

notoriously resistant to change of any kind, let alone the avalanche of change which is rapidly spreading to the furthermost corners of the world. Modernity, if we take this to mean the transformation of European societies in the industrial revolution and the Age of Enlightenment, redefined the place of the Christian denominations which emerged from the Reformation in societies that eventually became, to varying degrees, democratic or republican. It was taken as axiomatic until recently that this entailed the 'secularisation' of society and the consequent 'privatisation' of religious convictions as faith receded into the sphere of individual 'preference'. In the face of tumultuous developments on the global religious scene, such as the reinvigoration of Islam, the popularity of Buddhism and the rediscovery of indigenous religion, the secularisation thesis is being revised.[7]

Though secularity and the separation of church and state became the defining characteristics of 'modern' societies, in the West but also in Asia and Africa, it by no means follows that *global* civil society will automatically be secular, something that Western media and academic elites have yet to grasp. The dynamics of an inchoate, indeed chaotic world-wide civic space maintained by electronic social media without any overarching global government to moderate it seem to be having the effect of unleashing the best and the worst in the world's religions, giving free rein to every conceivable kind of fundamentalism but also to genuinely new and hopeful 'ecumenical' developments, notwithstanding the protests of those who loudly maintain that the elimination of religion altogether would bring us a giant step closer to solving the world's problems. This sets the parameters for the following investigation: Is a world theology feasible, is the world society which would be its context viable, and, if both questions can be answered in the affirmative, how would one go about constructing such a globalised theology?

World Theology?

Each identifiable religious tradition now has no other option than to

---

7. Notably by one of its main proponents, Peter Berger, *The Desecularization of the World* (Grand Rapids: Eerdmans, 1999); see also the magisterial re-reading of European intellectual history by Charles Taylor, *A Secular Age* (Cambridge, MA, and London: Belknap Press of Harvard University Press, 2007).

address these dramatic developments by drawing on its own time-hallowed resources—but in voluntary cooperation with others, no longer alone. In the new situation it is inconceivable that any one religious tradition could define all the others on its own terms and assert that it alone possessed the truth that would be the salvation of all humanity and the earth itself. Yet precisely this is what they have all traditionally done and continue to do. Therein lies the dilemma at the heart of any attempt to create a global theology. Indeed, this unhappy state of affairs has drawn alongside the problem of evil and the claims of rationalism as the third great objection to religion as such. These peremptory assertions now need to be substantiated.

In the case of Christianity, the core doctrines of incarnation (the assumption by Godself in the person of God's Son of the full humanity of the man Jesus of Nazareth) and redemption (the death of Jesus as a propitiatory sacrifice offered to the Father on behalf of sinful humanity) are constructed in such a way that they present themselves as definitive and unsurpassable, superseding every other revelation, whether historical or conceivable. What God reveals is not an additional insight into religious truth but Truth itself, Godself. As Karl Barth, in a stroke of theological genius, concluded, only faith, as a response to this revelation gifted by divine grace, can work salvation; everything else, including the ritual and institutional paraphernalia of the Christian churches, is 'religion' and amounts to human presumptuousness, an affront to the divine transcendence. It is only when one encounters attempts to develop this *Offenbarungspositivismus* ('revelational positivism'), as it has been called, in a missionary context, as in the work of Hendrik Kraemer—not to mention the single-minded proselytism of Evangelical, Pentecostal or Adventist missionaries, often supported from North America, in the Pacific Islands, Africa and South America—that its full incongruity becomes apparent.[8]

That this is not specifically a Protestant phenomenon is shown by Vatican pronouncements such as *Dominus Iesus* (2000), which by reaffirming the uniqueness and unicity of Christ and the (Catholic) Church as the sole means of salvation threaten to undo decades of patient interfaith theology and dialogue based on *Nostra Aetate* and

---

8. Hendrik Kraemer, *The Christian Message in a Non-Christian World* (London: Harper, 1938).

other documents of the Second Vatican Council (1962-1965).⁹ This is mainly because they view the situation exclusively from a Christian-Catholic standpoint, generally without any acknowledgement that other religions might have something to contribute, though one can also find a cautious admission of the necessity for dialogue as a component of evangelisation. Attempts to modify this stance by 'inclusivist' theologies which subsume other religions under the Christian scheme of salvation (Karl Rahner) or explicitly 'pluralist' proposals which would equalise and relativise the religions while maintaining their distinctiveness (John Hick) have not met with general acceptance.[10]

It may help us come to terms with this unsatisfactory situation if we Christians stand back for a moment from our own preoccupations and take account of the ways in which other religious traditions are beginning to confront similar problems in the same global context. It is by no means unusual for the 'primal' traditions of indigenous peoples to assume that they and they alone have been bequeathed the wisdom and prowess to dominate all others; indeed, there are cases in which their word for 'human beings' is the same as their word for 'our people', as is often the case in Melanesia. In the new context of mobility and rapid communication, however, indigenous peoples are finding that they have much in common, which gives them a basis for cooperation in securing their rights to land and humane treatment. But their traditional attitudes to 'others'—strangers and enemies—show how radically human it is to attribute exceptional status to 'our' group.

In the case of Muslims there is often a quite unselfconscious assumption that the Prophet was vouchsafed the final revelation of the way believers should live, superseding all others whether past,

---

9. See JD May, 'Catholic Fundamentalism: Some Implications of *Dominus Iesus* for Dialogue and Peacemaking', in *Horizons* 28 (2001): 271-293.
10. See Gavin D'Costa, *Theology and Religious Pluralism* (Oxford: Blackwell, 1986) for extensive critical discussion of Barth, Rahner and Hick—though D'Costa's position continues to evolve, see *The Meeting of Religions and the Trinity* (Edinburgh: T&T Clark, 2000)—and for reconfiguration and expansion of possible positions, Paul Knitter, *Introducing Theologies of Religions* (Maryknoll: Orbis Books, 2002). Perry Schmidt-Leukel, *Gott ohne Grenzen. Eine christliche und pluralistische Theologie der Religionen* (Gütersloh: Gütersloher Verlagshaus, 2005), maintains an uncompromisingly pluralist stance.

present or future, so that questions of comparison and relative validity do not really arise. With these convictions Muslims can usually find their place in the pluralist mix of secular societies with only minor irritation in matters such as diet or dress, but movements such as the Wahhabi Islam emanating from Saudi Arabia give this innocent absolutism a much more sinister cast, even to the extent of denying the status of Muslim to coreligionists who do not conform to its strict standards and calling on all true Muslims to wage violent *jihad* on infidels.

There is much more to be said, however, about the capacity of Islam to participate in a truly global theology. It is not generally realised that throughout the Middle Ages Muslims were much better informed about other religions and more objective in their judgements of them than Christians.[11] The emergence of Islam was 'frightening' for Christians, who regarded it as a particularly perverse heresy—for Luther, on a par with the Papacy![12] In its early history Islam was progressively politicised and ideologised as it became a force for social order and was thus intertwined with the state, so that the originating vision (*al-dīn*) was reduced to institutionalised Islam, and Islam was reduced to *sharīʿa*.[13] The present-day revival of Islam is itself a response to globalisation, but the ubiquity of modern communications media has created a 'global *ummah*', a virtual worldwide Islamic community, resulting in a 'polemical spiral' which is 'playing havoc in cyberspace'.[14]

It may seem surprising that quite intransigent attitudes to other religions have been commonplace in Buddhism, despite its reputation

---

11. See Lloyd Ridgeon and Perry Schmidt-Leukel, editors' introduction, *Islam and Inter-Faith Relations* (London: SCM Press, 2007), 3, citing the view of Harold Coward and referring to more detailed research by Jacques Waardenburg. I shall refer to this series of lectures and responses frequently as an example of the kind of collaboration that is now becoming possible.
12. See Martin Bauschke, 'A Christian View of Islam', Ridgeon and Schmidt-Leukel, *Islam and Inter-Faith Relations*, 138–140.
13. Jacques Waardenburg, 'Islam in a World of Diverse Faiths: A Historian's View', in Ridgeon and Schmidt-Leukel, *Islam and Inter-Faith Relations*, 17–32, 24–25; 'Response to Aydin', 58, referring to Mahmut Aydin, 'Islam and Diverse Faiths: A Muslim View', 33–54 in the same volume.
14. Ataullah Siddiqui, 'A Muslim View of Christianity', in Ridgeon and Schmidt-Leukel, *Islam and Inter-Faith Relations*, 121–136, 128. See also Olivier Roy, *Globalised Islam: The Search for a New Ummah* (London: C Hurst, 2004).

for tolerance. On the contrary: historically, Buddhists have shown little or no interest in understanding or even acknowledging other traditions such as Islam or Chinese religion.[15] Theravada Buddhism has an inbuilt conviction that its *Dhamma* is the one and only sure way to liberation from the suffering (*dukkha*, more properly 'unsatisfactoriness', 'unease') endemic in the human condition, and the appalling violence which has characterised the conflict in Sri Lanka has been legitimised by this conviction, which fuses ethnic and religious superiority into one nationalistic amalgam, equally intolerant of Hindu-Tamil and Western-Christian otherness. The case of Buddhism is particularly discouraging because of the prominence of wisdom (*prajnā*) and compassion (*karunā*) in all its very diverse schools and its ideal of equanimity or even-mindedness (*upekkhā*) as a basis for rising above passion and prejudice in resolving conflict. It is perhaps the cultivation of a kind of sublime indifference that has sometimes led Buddhists, for example Japanese Zen masters and their followers in the time of imperialistic militarism before the Second World War, to obey the Emperor's command to take up arms without reflection, as an archer, a flower arranger or one performing the tea ceremony eliminates self and lets the action take its own course (as eminent an authority as DT Suzuki could say that Zen simply *is* religion, implying that nothing else is, a move as strikingly audacious as Karl Barth's).[16]

More progressive Buddhist thinkers such as Thich Nhat Hanh, the Dalai Lama and the Thai monk Buddhadāsa have explored the possibilities of a Buddhist 'inclusivism', utilising traditional concepts such as the all-inclusive 'one vehicle' (*ekayāna*) of the *Lotus Sūtra* or the theory of 'two truths', a transcendent truth (*paramārtha-satya*) which is knowable to liberated ones but inaccessible to reason, and a conventional truth (*samvrti-satya*) which is valid in the everyday life-world constructed by language. The problem with such strategies is that they privilege Buddhism while denying that they do so, and

---

15. See the studies of Alexander Berzin, 'A Buddhist View of Islam', Ridgeon and Schmidt-Leukel, *Islam and Inter-Faith Relations*, 225–251, 227, 229, 230, 233; 'Buddhist-Christian Doctrinal Relations: Past, Present and Future', in *Buddhist Attitudes to Other Religions,* edited Perry Schmidt-Leukel by (St Ottilien: EOS Verlag, 2008), 212–236.
16. See Brian Victoria, *Zen at War* (New York: Weatherhill, 1997); on Suzuki, 104–110.

the problem is compounded by many Buddhists' lack of awareness that their inherited traditions are culturally conditioned.[17]

In the context of replying to the then Cardinal Ratzinger's *Dominus Iesus* this assumption that one's own uniqueness implies superiority over everyone else was well named 'meliorism' (from *melior,* 'better').[18] But once this is acknowledged it at least puts us all on an equal footing in confronting the problem of how we can come together spiritually and collaborate theologically while not surrendering whatever it is that gives us our religious identity and grounds us in our traditions. The framework of secular societies based on liberal tolerance—and indifference to what people believe as long as they do not claim exclusive status—is something quite different, invaluable though it is as an achievement that took the sting out of post-Reformation religious strife. In the future global civil society, as indeed in the increasingly multi-cultural societies of virtually all continents and civilisations, this will not be enough; it may not even be viable. A generalised tolerance, invaluable as it is as the framework for civil rights such as 'freedom of expression' or 'religious liberty', must progress to the point where it becomes explicit engagement with one another's deepest convictions. Even 'dialogue', difficult and necessary as it is, does not capture the degree of urgency and the level of challenge entailed by religious collaboration, not just in practical cooperation but also in theological reflection.

World Society?

It has become *de rigeur* to dismiss multiculturalism as a failed project, most recently in Britain and Germany, but increasingly in Australia as well. Perhaps it is the '-ism' that puts people off, but whatever we call it, we have no choice, in my view, but to learn to live with culturally and religiously different 'others', from the streets

---

17. See Schmidt-Leukel, *Buddhist Attitudes*, especially the contributions of Kristin Beise Kiblinger, 'Buddhist Stances Towards Others: Types, Examples, Considerations', 24–46, and John Makransky, 'Buddhist Inclusivism: Reflections Toward a Contemporary Buddhist Theology of Religions', 47–68; see also Kiblinger, *Buddhist Inclusivism: Attitudes Towards Religious Others* (Burlington, Vt: Ashgate, 2005).
18. Ottmar Fuchs, 'Plädoyer für eine ebenso dissensfähige wie ebenbürtige Ökumene', Michael Rainer, ed., *"Dominus Iesus": Anstössige Wahrheit oder anstössige Kirche?* (Münster-Hamburg-London: LIT Verlag, 2001), 169–195.

and neighbourhoods of our local communities to the emerging global community of peoples, nations and states. If we do not make this considerable ecumenical effort, the inevitable conflicts tend to become violent and nation-states ensconce themselves behind restrictive immigration laws and the rejection of refugees. When racially motivated violence is reinforced by absolutist religious convictions, it can become ineradicable. To advocate an ecumenical alternative to the religious sanctioning of ethnic conflict and economic rivalry is thus not mere idealism: it is radical realism.

Western liberal societies, following the pattern established above for the religions, tend to take for granted that their kinds of polity set the norm for societies everywhere, and that the coming global civil society will inevitably follow this pattern and be judged by this norm. But this assumption begs two questions. Having spent all my life in democracies of one kind or another, I am keenly aware of what a privilege it is to live in a society where basic rights are respected and freedoms granted, and where a certain level of prosperity and security is attainable by all. But there are other ways of achieving these goals than Westminster-style parliamentary democracy or presidential-style republican constitutions. If the colonisation of most of the world by Western powers had not proceeded so brutally and rapidly, there may well have been time for alternative models of political society to emerge, and the outcome of the recent upheavals across the Arab world will be extremely interesting in this regard. Enormously important as it was to establish genuinely pluralist societies in which there is room for a variety of ideological and religious convictions, without the need to suppress dissent and with mechanisms for the transfer of power according to the expressed will of the people, and indispensable as it was under the circumstances obtaining in post-Reformation Europe or post-independence India for such societies to be secular, their limitations are exposed as the pressures of globalisation increase. The rationality that sustains science offers little help in solving the human and ecological problems it has created; the ideal of tolerance appears helpless in the face of religious extremism and uncompromising terrorism; and the granting of equal rights to women, ethnic minorities and refugees is by no means complete.[19]

---

19. On this and what follows, see JD May, 'Alternative a Dio? Le religioni nella sfera

The second assumption that needs to be questioned is that a future global civil society, if indeed it comes about, will be secular and democratic on the same European pattern. Difficult as it still is to discern its contours, such a society would have no highest authority, no government which could legislate bindingly and to which appeals for justice could be made (the vicissitudes of the United Nations, indispensable as this beleaguered organisation is, only underline its inadequacy in these respects). Nor would there be any 'outsiders' in relation to which a sense of identity could be maintained: we would all be 'insiders', busily marking off our identities over against others but at the same time striving to construct some kind of global identity.[20] This, as far as one can see, would be an unstable amalgam of inherited identities in a constant state of interaction, with a strong secular component but undoubtedly incorporating powerful religious currents and communities. My point is that a constructed secular framework of ideological neutrality and religious tolerance will no longer be adequate to contain these. It will be necessary for there to be a substantive, not merely a formal pluralism, an interactive pluralism which will eventually change the participants. In the terms proposed by systems theory: no one of the many functional subsystems which make up a society will be able to define and represent this unstable whole, neither *one* of the religions nor *one* of the dominant ideologies.[21] No such totalising system could thematise the emergent whole and make a plausible claim to be normative for it. The only social subsystem that has come close to achieving this is the market, with economics as its 'theology' and all-pervading 'economism' as its normative value.[22] The poverty of such a scenario was brutally exposed by the global financial crisis

---

pubblica globale', Antonio Autiero, editor, *Teologia nella città, teologia per la città* (Bologna: Edizioni Dehoniane, 2005), 95-109; JD May, 'God in Public: The Religions in Pluralist Societies', in *Bijdragen: International Journal in Philosophy and Theology*, 64/3 (2003): 249-264.

20. On this intriguing prospect see Peter Beyer, *Religion and Globalization* (London: Sage Publications, 1994), 38.
21. See Peter Beyer, *Religions in Global Society* (London and New York: Routledge, 2006), with reference to systems theory as developed by Talcott Parsons and applied to religion by Niklas Luhmann.
22. See David R Loy, 'The Religion of the Market', in *Journal of the American Academy of Religion* 65/2 (1997): 275-290.

of 2008-2009, and it is manifested in a different way as China rises to global economic prominence while denying and suppressing the spiritual heritage of its great religious traditions.

By now the problems these developments pose for theology, whether Christian or otherwise, should be apparent. In the world order—or perhaps disorder?—I have sketched there is no place in principle for exclusivistic, dogmatic worldviews of any kind, yet what we see in practice is a proliferation and intensification of them—and by no means only religious ones. In ways that are yet to be fully understood, this is a response to the pressures of globalisation, but it does not mean that the collective religious convictions inherited from traditions great and small should be relativised and neutered, so that they become mere options in the supermarket of ideas. How to achieve this in the new situation is the ecumenical challenge of our time. It implies that we must disabuse ourselves of the idea that the ecumenical is the soft option for liberals and agnostics who are not particularly committed to any faith but are prepared to entertain a selection of them at a safe distance. The kind of ecumenism I am proposing is one where religious convictions do not simply evaporate in a general climate of tolerance but strengthen as they engage with the equally strong convictions of religious others, coexisting with them and interacting with them until such time as ways can be found to sustain together shared visions of hope for the human future and agreed ethical bases for action in the present.[23] It may well be that such a pluralistic coexistence is a more realistic goal than a prematurely constructed ultimate commonality which only intellectual elites can fully grasp.[24] Not all would put it as bluntly as Majid Tehranian: 'The new Global Civilization demands a new faith. That faith has to transcend all existing faiths.'[25] If a Muslim can assert this, then Christian theologians have much to ponder. One thing, at any rate, is clear: if we are even to approximate to these goals, we must all change the way we do theology.

---

23. See JD May, 'Ethic of Survival or Vision of Hope? The Aim of Interreligious Dialogue', in *Dharma World* 29 (Sept–Oct 2002): 25–28; JD May, 'Die ökumenische Alternative. Die eine bewohnte Erde neu denken', in *Salzburger Theologische Zeitschrift*, 14/2 (2010): 187–202.
24. See Chakravarti Ram-Prasad, 'Response to Engineer', in Ridgeon and Schmidt-Leukel, *Islam and Inter-Faith Relations*, 209.
25. Majid Tehranian, 'A Muslim View of Buddhism', in Ridgeon and Schmidt-Leukel, *Islam and Inter-Faith Relations*, 213–224, 216.

Towards Collaborative Theology

Many who are working intensively in the field of interreligious studies are beginning to realise that we need to go beyond objective surveys of the ways the religions represent themselves in the public sphere to the point where they begin to engage with one another theologically. In the case of Christianity and Islam, Martin Bauschke can assert:

> In face of fundamentalist demagogues both sides have the responsibility to create an alternative to . . . a 'theology of hate', that is, a *theology of reconciliation and friendship between Christians and Muslims*. This theology needs to be developed jointly and, being a common Christian-Muslim theology, it is therefore different from either a 'Christian view of Islam' or a 'Muslim view of Christianity' as we have presented here.[26]

Any such venture, of course, has presuppositions which are only just beginning to be explored; as Bauschke continues: 'In order to develop a Christian-Muslim theology of reconciliation and friendship we need a *common Christian-Muslim hermeneutics of their sacred Scriptures*.'[27]

Remarking on how teachings such as 'skilful means' (*kauśalya-upāya*) have allowed Buddhists to assimilate viewpoints from other schools while maintaining the doctrinal superiority of their own, John Makransky acknowledges that 'Buddhist traditions of Asia, and now of the West, are products of the recurrent, fresh integration of non-Buddhist religious and cultural elements into new Buddhist frameworks.'[28]

Agreeing with Catholic theologian Jacques Dupuis that religions need one another in order to plumb the depths of their own truths, Makransky goes on:

---

26. Bauschke, 'Response to Siddiqui', in Ridgeon and Schmidt-Leukel, *Islam and Inter-Faith Relations*, 159 (emphasis in original).
27. Bauschke, 'Response to Siddiqui', in Ridgeon and Schmidt-Leukel, *Islam and Inter-Faith Relations*, 161 (emphasis in original).
28. Makransky, 'Buddhist Inclusivism', in Schmidt-Leukel, *Buddhist Attitudes*, 59.

> It is not just that Buddhahood is speaking itself through other religious traditions so as to include them as lower levels of preparation on the ladder to Buddhist enlightenment. Rather Buddhists *need* the wisdom of religious others to help disclose to them what lies outside of the historically conditioned limitations of their own tradition, to help them receive *more* of the truth that frees, perhaps sometimes in surprising and unexpected ways . . . [29]

In developing what he unapologetically calls a Buddhist *theology*, notwithstanding the absence of a personal God in traditional Buddhist thought, Makransky freely acknowledges the influence on him of Christian colleagues such as the Jesuit Francis Clooney, whose essays in a Hindu-Christian 'comparative theology' have excited much interest.[30]

These few examples suffice to show that we are on the threshold of what I would want to call 'collaborative theology' in which the most fundamental presuppositions of each tradition would be debated across institutional boundaries in much the same way as doctrinal matters have been within the traditions, except that now, instead of being taken for granted as data of revelation or self-evident truths, these presuppositions would be mutually challenged at the deepest level. Only communication partners with a mature level of trust could undertake such a project. This might well take place in a spirit of competition, but even in the midst of conflict space needs to be made for this further reflection, for by expanding the context of conflict in this way and drawing on the deepest resources of each side even violent conflict can be resolved by the parties to the conflict themselves.[31] But, to borrow a remark of the recently

---

29. Makransky, 'Buddhist Inclusivism', in Schmidt-Leukel, *Buddhist Attitudes*, 64.
30. See John Makransky, *Buddhahood Embodied: Sources of Controversy in India and Tibet* (Albany: SUNY Press, 1997); Francis Clooney, *Comparative Theology: Deep Learning Across Religious Borders* (Oxford: Wiley-Blackwell, 2010).
31. See Marc Gopin, *Between Eden and Armageddon: The Future of World Religions, Violence, and Peacemaking* (Oxford: Oxford University Press, 2000); *Holy War, Holy Peace: How Religion Can Bring Peace to the Middle East* (Oxford: Oxford University Press, 2002). Just as Gopin has seen this potential realised in the Middle East, I have observed it in Northern Ireland.

deceased former Irish prime minister Garret FitzGerald, 'That's all very well in practice, but how would it work in theory?' The hard intellectual work of reconciling fundamentally opposed religious viewpoints remains. It is no solution to achieve this in the abstract in ways which actual religious believers cannot accept. One does not compose hymns to abstractions, nor can they console the grieving or inspire hope in the suffering. The task for collaborative theology is not just to 'mention', but also to 'use' religious language in all its particularity in ways which gradually expand its field of reference so that it is understood beyond the cultural boundaries of determinate traditions. This is not just a matter of finding 'common ground'; indeed, 'common' ground only too often turns out to reflect the basic doctrines of one of the parties to the discussion.

One way of approaching this problem would be to explore symbolic equivalences between the ruling metaphors which govern the 'deep structures' of each tradition's language. Much work has already been done along these lines, for example, correlating the Christian concept of God with the Buddhist *Dharma*; the Kingdom or Reign of God in Christian tradition with Nirvana as the Buddhist Ultimate which is nevertheless non-dual with contingent existence in time; or the Trinity-Incarnation complex with the Three Bodies of the Buddha (*trikāya*) and the Three Characteristics of existence (*tilakkhana*).[32] There is also much potential in concepts such as hope, compassion and reconciliation.[33] In many such cases one comes

---

32. For some preliminary attempts at this, with further references, see Schmidt-Leukel, *Gott ohne Grenzen*, 455–461, 466–477 on the work of pioneering thinkers Lynn de Silva and Abe Masao; JD May, 'Creator Spirit: A Narrative Theology of the Trinity in Interreligious Relations', in *Trinity and Salvation: Theological, Spiritual and Aesthetic Perspectives*, edited by Declan Marmion and Gesa Thiessen (Oxford, Bern et al: Peter Lang, 2009), 161–18; JD May, 'Schöpfung erzählen. Möglichkeiten narrativer Buddhologie – auch für die Christologie', in *Mystik – Herausforderung und Inspiration. Gotthard Fuchs zum 70. Geburtstag*, edited by Thomas Pröpper, Michael Raske, Jürgen Werbick (Ostfildern: Matthias-Grünewald-Verlag, 2008), 128–138.

33. For some further experiments along these lines, see JD May, 'May Buddhists Hope? A Christian Enquiry' in *Loss and Hope: Global, Interreligious and Interdisciplinary Perspectives*, edited by Peter Admirand (London: Bloomsbury, 2014, forthcoming); 'Sympathy and Empathy: The Compassionate Bodhisattva and the Love of Christ', *Crossroad Discourses Between Christianity and Culture*, edited by Jerald D Gort, Henry Jansen, and Wessel Stoker (Amsterdam and New York: Editions Rodopi, 2010), 395–411.

to the realisation that Buddhism and Christianity, in their most fundamental aspects, are at one and the same time—sometimes in respect of one and the same question—radically different and radically the same, notwithstanding the Buddhists' reservations about the separate existence of a Creator God, the personal nature of God, or indeed the reality of a personal Self. One glimpses the possibility of re-tracing intellectually the ground already staked out by Christian and Buddhist spiritual practitioners who are open to dialogue.

Another line of approach, which perhaps offers more immediately attainable results, is the path of ethics, where agreement can often quickly be reached about basic principles and practices whose contexts and motivations may nevertheless differ considerably. The differences involved often turn out to be more cultural than doctrinal, for example, in Japanese attitudes to contraception and abortion, which are generally supported by Buddhists but would be rejected by many Christians. Questions of human rights and social responsibility confront us with the widely differing views of the person in the two traditions, yet the Socially Engaged Buddhism which has now emerged, especially in Southeast Asia, shares practical goals consonant with those of Christian Liberation Theology.[34] Now that ecology is being seen as an ethical issue, involving in some way as yet difficult to grasp for Western traditions the 'rights' of species and of nature itself, Christian thinkers such as Paul Knitter and John B Cobb have found much to ponder in the Buddhist conception of universal interconnectedness of all components of reality (*paticcasamuppāda*).[35] The trans-theistic Buddhist perspective still leaves Christians with puzzling questions: Are Buddhists in a position to take history seriously, and does the elimination of the individual self attenuate the moral responsibility contingent upon individual existence in time? Yet in practice such issues are very often resolved, suggesting that their resolution in theory is attainable.

---

34. See JD May, 'What do Socially Engaged Buddhists and Christian Liberation Theologians Have to Say to One Another?', in *Dialogue*, 21 (1994), 1–18, with special reference to the work of Aloysius Pieris SJ of Sri Lanka and Sulak Sivaraksa of Thailand.
35. See Paul F Knitter, *One Earth, Many Religions: Multifaith Dialogue and Global Responsibility* (Maryknoll: Orbis Books, 1995); John B Cobb, *Sustainability: Economics, Ecology and Justice* (Maryknoll: Orbis Books, 1992); JD May, '"Rights of the Earth" and "Care for the Earth": Two Paradigms for a Buddhist-Christian Ecological Ethic', in *Horizons*, 21 (1994): 48–61.

What seems to be called for in the globalisation of theology, illustrated here all too briefly by reference to Buddhist and Christian collaboration, is something like the philosophical conversion undergone by the Japanese Buddhist philosopher Tanabe Hajime (1885–1962) under the impact of Zen Buddhism's helplessness in the face of imperialistic militarism at the height of the Second World War. It led him to resign his chair at Kyoto University and withdraw to the mountains, only emerging when he had fashioned what he called a 'metanoetics', a turning around of Buddhist-inspired philosophy reminiscent of Christian *metanōia* but resolutely intellectual, not moral, in conception.[36]

In the flux of global communication in the emerging global public sphere religious thinking becomes elusive, which possibly explains why people of faith—in all faiths—turn to varieties of fundamentalism as a refuge from the kind of radical questioning hinted at here.[37] The examples given above are taken from only one set of interreligious relationships, though surely one of the most intellectually and spiritually challenging; in principle, and increasingly in practice, such mutual questioning is opening up among all religious traditions with more or less determinate doctrinal structures. These exchanges are taking place against the background of a global fusion of philosophies, cultures and languages, and if they are still somewhat inchoate, they certainly transcend the sterile debates sparked off by the so-called 'new atheism'. They may be daunting for the more doctrinally developed religions such as Christianity and Buddhism, in which the questioning of fundamentals appears to threaten whole doctrinal edifices erected over the centuries to safeguard central beliefs. But those who have entered into them with openness to new insights and trust in their own fidelity and their partners' integrity regularly report that they have been liberated from culturally conditioned narrowness and inspired to renewed faithfulness to what

---

36. See Makoto Ozaki, *Introduction to the Philosophy of Tanabe: According to the English Translation of the Seventh Chapter of the* Demonstration of Christianity (Amsterdam: Editions Rodopi; Grand Rapids: Eerdmans, 1990). Warning: Tanabe's thought is bafflingly difficult, even for those versed in the thought of the Kyoto School!
37. This line of thought is developed, with often colorful examples from the Australasian context, by Gary Bouma, *Being Faithful in Diversity* (Adelaide: ATF Press, 2011).

really matters in their respective heritages.[38] The outcome of such reciprocal engagement is not knowable in advance; to embark on it demands a special kind of courage, which is more likely to be found among lonely pioneers than the hierarchies of religious authority. But if theology—now of an intercultural and interreligious type[39]—is to keep pace with the breathtaking developments of globalisation, the construction of such theology, shared among all traditions willing to participate, would seem to be the true ecumenical alternative to ethnocentrism and religious absolutism.

---

38. One of the most remarkable testimonies to such a conversion through dialogue is Paul F Knitter's recent book, *Without Buddha I Could Not be a Christian* (Oxford: One World, 2009).
39. See JD May and Linda Hogan, 'Visioning Ecumenics as Intercultural, Inter-religious, and Public Theology', in *Concilium: From World Mission to Inter-religious Witness*, edited by Linda Hogan, Solange Lefebvre, Norbert Hintersteiner, and Felix Wilfred (London: SCM, 2011), 70-81.

Contemporary Globalisation and Local Struggles for Social Justice

Rowan Ireland

Three decades ago, the mantra 'Think global, act local' was current among activists for social justice and Third World development. Back then, the mantra often encapsulated the judgments that justice and the just resided in the local (potentially at least) and that encroaching global forces threatened local struggles for social justice. To think global meant, among other things, to know your enemy. This was especially the case where the local struggle was predicated on two strategic notions. First, the communitarian notion that social justice would and should be achieved 'from below', in and through the struggles of local communities. Second, the notion (condensed in Paulo Freire's concept of 'conscientisation'[1]) that local communities for justice would develop as their members learned to identify, name and voice their own experiences of injustice, and take collective action to address them. Globalisation was the enemy because, in its economic forms (described below) it destroyed local communities, and in its cultural forms (also outlined below) it distorted and drowned out the 'voices of the voiceless' as they attempted to name their experiences.

As the apostrophised phrases might remind us, the communitarian and conscientisation strategies were exemplified in the ideals and practice of the Latin American Basic Church Communities, the CEBs, to use their Spanish and Portuguese acronym. Among CEBs-

---

1. Paulo Freire, *Pedagogy of the Oppressed* (New York: Continuum, 2007). The book, well-known to educators around the world, first appeared in English in 1970. The word 'conscientisation' is an awful neologism in English. Many prefer the phrase 'awareness-raising'.

inspired activists for social justice in the 1980s, local expressions of globalisation were seen both to be root causes of social injustice, and to subvert their twin strategies for journeys toward the justice and peace Kingdom of God.[2] In this paper, which explores the impact of the several processes of contemporary globalisation on local struggles for social justice, the central case is a residents' association in a Brazilian shantytown (*favela*). This association had grown out of a CEB whose members sought social justice for their *favela* as an integral expression of their Christian faith. A key issue in this study, which the author has been conducting for twenty-five years, is whether globalisation has been as uniformly destructive of this sort of local action for social justice as it was often conceived to be.

Over the years of the study, globalisation and its connections with local struggles have come to be understood in more nuanced terms than they were at the beginning. Globalisation now appears as a set of contradictory processes. It looms large as a threat to local struggles, but also provides resources and opportunity to local communities. The contradictions, including the lineaments of 'good' globalisation illustrated in the case study, are further revealed in a review of 'transnational social movement organisations' (TSMOs) which have become integral aspects of contemporary globalisation over the last three decades. This acknowledgment of the contradictions and good aspects is not meant to obscure continuing prejudicial impacts of globalisation on local projects for social justice. Far from it: the paper takes off with an outline of arguments about negative impacts by a range of social scientists. However, the aim of this paper is neither to praise, nor condemn globalisation (at this point the latter is akin to condemning electricity, as the Liberation theologian Gustavo Guttiérez is reported to have said). Rather, the aim is to illuminate the global context which local movements and associations must understand and address (as they do, increasingly) if they are to survive and harness the opportunities of globalisation in their pursuit of social justice.

---

2. See for a brief example, Leonardo Boff, 'Liberation Theology and Globalisation' written for *Inter Press Service* in 1999, and available on the web at www.vlny.cz/christianpeace/cpc/info/wn001a.htm. Last consulted on 1/04/2012.

Negative impacts of Contemporary Globalisation

Globalisation, the complex of processes whereby all corners of the globe are increasingly linked by trade, communication networks, flows of information, migration and political interaction, has a very long history. Since the 1970s, however, it has become more and more evident that qualitative turns are being made in that history, so that we have to use a qualifier like 'contemporary' to indicate both the new forms, the increased pace, and the heightened intensity of globalisation over the last four decades. Many forces—economic, political, technological and cultural—combine to drive contemporary globalisation. Among them is the continuing informational revolution through which space and time are compressed in the flows of information and capital on the web. The constant and instantaneous flows of the web constitute an entirely new global marketplace for the exchanges of the capitalist system.

The global marketplace exists in virtual time and space, but it is real in its impacts on daily life in every corner of the globe. The new global capitalist market place operates according to the old logic of capitalist markets, but is increasingly free of mediation and modification in the national political economies in which capitalist markets remained embedded for much of the twentieth century. That means that the global capitalist market, while it does not destroy the nation-state system, increasingly over-rides it. In turn, that means that global capitalism operates ever more free from the political, cultural and moral constraints placed on it in countries like Australia which were able, in the twentieth century, to develop policies and regulations to modify the operation of markets in the name of social justice, welfare, and public goods.

Let us consider the charges against contemporary globalisation under headings of the several forms, economic, political and cultural, in which it is experienced. Many of the charges against are directed at *economic* globalisation in the form of large trans-national corporations, allied global institutions like the IMF, and national governments that do the bidding of both. These entities often work together to undermine, destroy or dismantle national institutions and local movements that seek to modify, or propose alternatives to, the free operation of global markets. The allegations include charges that economic globalisation, as promoted by these agencies under the rubrics of 'market reform', 'structural adjustment programs' and 'growth maximisation', subverts trade unions; wages war on squatters' movements struggling for urban land and settlement rights; destroys indigenous groups which stand in the way of transnational mining projects. These are examples, often posited, but also amply demonstrated, of the prejudicial impact of *economic* globalisation on collective action for rights and social justice.

More generally, contemporary globalisation in its economic manifestations refers also to the global diffusion of neo-liberal economic policies—for example, cutbacks in state budgets for social services, privatization of public enterprises, deregulation of economies, and ruthless pursuit of free-market 'reforms'. These, singly and in concert, directly and indirectly, are involved in accounts of the de-mobilisation of grassroots movements for citizens' rights and social justice in Latin America and elsewhere in the developing world [3]. Trade unions, which, whatever their faults, have been involved in the defence of workers' rights and struggles for a just wage, have been a particular target of alliances formed between large multi-national corporations and national governments in the name of freeing global trade and local labour markets from institutional constraints. That has been the case not only over there in developing countries, but right here in well-developed Australia. The union-curbing policies and actions of the Howard Government, including the 1998 waterfront dispute, have been sheeted home to the conjunction of corporate globalisation strategies and the Government's commitment to free-market, neo-liberal policies.[4]

Political globalisation also stands accused. This refers to the processes whereby the power to determine public policy is sucked out of local and national institutions and becomes invested in the likes of virtually constituted 'mid-Atlantic boardrooms'. Increasingly, as political globalisation advances, the decisions that shape our labour

---

3. Ton Salman, 'The Diffident Movement: The Role of Generation and Gender in the Vicissitudes of the Chilean Shantytown Organizations 1973-1990', in *Latin American Perspectives*, 21/3 (1994): 8 31. John Gledhill, 'Citizenship and the social geography of deep neo-liberalization', in *Anthropolgica*, 47/1 (2005): 81–100, especially 90–93.
4. John Wiseman, 'Trade Union Solidarity: The Australian Waterfront, 1998', in *Protest and Globalisation: Prospects for Transnational Solidarity*, edited by James Goodman (Annandale, NSW: Pluto Press Australia, 2002), 170-181.

markets, our cities, our material and social well-being, are made not in particular places by identifiable, and potentially accountable power-holders, but in the flows of the worldwide web itself[5]. Several consequences include failure of social movements pursuing social justice aims when the formally constituted legislatures and executives they target turn out to be powerless to effect change. Support for the movements fades away once the demonstrations, petitions, and other well-tried means of influencing power holders which they deploy turn out to be fruitless.

Then, less obviously perhaps, *cultural* globalisation may also undermine movements and institutions striving for rights and social justice. Like other forms of globalisation, the cultural form is itself a complex of processes. It includes the development of a transnational corporate system for the production of popular culture (the Sony world music empire comes to mind); the development of global media for the distribution of popular cultures and news (the Murdoch empire is an instance); and the development of what John Street[6] has called 'global multiculturalism'. Alone, or in concert, these elements of cultural globalisation have effectively detached sections of local populations (for example youth) from their local cultural roots and incorporated them in homogenized global sub-cultures of desire, consumption and life-style. In this way, cultural globalisation has been shown to be involved in the generational fragmentation of local communities that were once the bases for the mobilisation of young and old for collective action for social justice[7].

At the same time, global media stand accused of promoting a culture of consumerism on a global scale. As members of particular societies are variously seduced (the better off) or forced (the poor) into consumerist culture, they abandon life-long commitments, loyalties, and collective goals, to become individual consumers out

---

5. Manuel Castells, *The Rise of the Network Society* (Malden MA: Blackwell, 1996), 5-27
6. John Street, 'Global Culture, Local Culture', in *Leisure Studies*, 12/3 (1993): 191-201.
7. For a Brazilian example see Geert Banck, 'Mass Communication and Urban Contest in Brazil: Some Reflections on Lifestyle and Class', in *Bulletin of Latin American Research*, 13/1 (1995): 45-60. For an Australian example see Kevin McDonald, *Struggles for Subjectivity: Identity, Action and Youth Experience* (Cambridge: Cambridge University Press, 1999).

to satisfy unlimited media-nurtured desires. Life itself becomes a series of short-term projects and tactics for survival or advancement in societies based on an 'aesthetic of consumption'.[8] As a culture of consumerism becomes dominant in a supposedly democratic society, its citizens in effect, become mere inhabitants. The better off abandon the notion of collective responsibility for individual (still less social class) misfortune, and the poor become a nuisance underclass of 'failed consumers', undeserving of collective concern. The poor, frustrated and excluded, may explode from time to time in destructive protest, but lose opportunity, capacity and will to take organised collective action for social and economic alternatives. Former concerned citizens lose the desire, and the skills to struggle for and maintain public goods like universal education, public health and other services. In this way, the globally diffused culture of consumerism, according to Zygmunt Bauman and others, helps dissolve local societies in the operations of global markets.

Finally, cultural globalisation refers to the global diffusion of neo-liberalism as the prevailing common sense among economists and policy-makers. As neo-liberalism has become what Michel Foucault called a 'truth regime' around the world, it has become easier for powers-that-be to dismiss the critiques and alternatives advanced by social justice advocates as economic non-sense, as opposed to the sound common sense that rules, as true-believers say it should, in a free-market world.

In the Brazilian case-study that follows, the three modes of globalization—economic, political and cultural—may be seen to work negatively on a local struggle for justice and rights. But the case also displays creative address at the local level to the negative pressures of globalisation. Further, it bears witness to positive contributions from the global to the benefit of those struggling for justice and social alternatives at the local level. In this case, residents in a Brazilian shanty-town struggle for decent living conditions, and a say in urban policy-making. The story of their struggles illustrates some of the ambiguities of globalisation. On the one hand, we see connections between the various forms of globalisation and deprivation of shanty-town residents of their rights to land and

---

8. Zygmunt Bauman, *Work, Consumption, and the New Poor* (Philadelphia: Open University Press, 1998).

urban services, their access to the means to seek redress, and their ability to enact alternative futures. Thus it illustrates the impact of negative globalisation. On the other hand, as residents address their deprivations, we can see concomitants of globalisation equipping them with capacities and resources for the construction of their alternative city. This exemplifies positive globalisation.[9] In this case, and in the subsequent outline of the rise of Transnational Social Movement Organisations (TSMOs), we can see not only ambiguities but also the contradictions of globalisation. The notion of contradictions is used here to indicate that the very processes that curtail or even destroy local collective action for rights, social justice and alternative futures, may provide the incentives, opportunities and means for local agents to win some rounds, at least, in struggles against the forces of negative globalisation. Where negative globalisation would corral local activists so that they remain objects in the deep social, political and transformations they experience, positive globalisation allows their development as subjects or agents of their own histories, to a greater or lesser extent.

Globalisation and the struggle for urbanization in Jardim Oratório

In 1988,[10] the author commenced study of residents' associations in several *favelas* in three Brazilian cities. At the time, advocates of social justice and many social scientists were excited about new social movements of the poor in Brazil, and indeed in other Latin American societies. These movements appeared to challenge authoritarian military governments which committed themselves to discipline their populations, the poor especially, so as to maximise the advantages of the national economy in the global marketplace. Further, it was claimed, the movements pre-figured and generated deep and extensive social, economic and political transformations. Networks of *favela* residents' associations were seen as vital elements

---

9. A more accurate but long-winded way of expressing the point is to say that this is an instance of what might be called positive vectors in the complex of globalisation factors.
10. The year is significant. This was the year in which Brazil's new Constitution was approved by the Federal Legislature. It affirmed and elaborated democratic governance following the end of the military governments, 1964–1985.

in the new movements, along with groups of the rural poor struggling for land rights, a range of grassroots communities of the Catholic Church (the CEBs), and factory workers attempting to establish new types of trade unions.[11]

The aims of the *favela* residents' associations varied over time but typically involved a sequence of negotiations with local government. The first set aimed to achieve regularisation of tenure of occupied urban land. The second set sought 'urbanisation'—the provision of basic urban infrastructure, including adequate housing, water, sewerage and electricity connections *etcetera*. The residents' associations were claimed to be more than pressure groups. They were seen to progress from making demands on local government to experimenting with new forms of self-government. They organised various forms of cooperative projects, for example, house-construction, and campaigned for human rights through association networks. In other words, it was claimed that they advanced from being reactive to the immediate threats to survival facing residents in squatter settlements, to being proactive in the construction of new forms of urban living; and that they moved beyond an agenda of demands to an agenda of human rights. They were thought to prefigure deep social, political and economic changes produced by the disadvantaged poor.[12]

At the start of what has turned out to be a twenty year plus project, a major aim of fieldwork conducted in the favelas was to see whether the hopeful claims made about the *favela* associations were valid, and held over time. Were they so proactive and creative in the pursuit of social justice for favela residents? Was a new, viable form of participatory democracy being nurtured in them? A less hopeful scenario had to be considered by the researcher as he addressed these questions. In 1984, Manuel Castells had

---

11. Two of many articles arguing that something new and important was stirring in the urban popular movements are: Tilman Evers, 'Identity: The Hidden Side of New Social Movements in Latin America', in *New Social Movements and the State in Latin America*, edited by David Slater (Amsterdam: CEDLA Publications, 1985), 43-71. Scott Mainwaring and Eduardo Viola 'New Social Movements, Political Culture and Democracy: Brazil and Argentina in the 1980s', in *Telos*, 61 (Fall 1984): 17-54.

12. John Friedmann, 'The Dialectic of Reason', in *International Journal of Urban and Regional Research* 13/2 (1989): 217-236.

published a magisterial study of urban social movements that was pessimistic about the chances of success for urban squatters' movements in the dependent political economies of Latin America[13] In Castells' view, contemporary economic globalisation had created a chain of dependencies. National and political elites, dependent on transnational corporations for capital investment in industry, strove to provide cheap labour by allowing a flood of migrants into urban industrial areas without urban planning regulations or provision of housing and basic social services. At the same time, workers trying to protect the material and spatial basis of their way of life in squatter settlements had to maintain close patron-client ties in the elite-controlled political system, since the entire system of minimal service delivery on which they relied, albeit precariously, depended on state agencies. In Castells' words, 'the squatters, the state and the informal economy, in intimate relation with the formal sector, are elements of the same system: the dependent city, the dependent state, the dependent economy'.[14] In the dependent city, the hopeful claims about squatters' associations would be negated, for the dependent city is a city effectively denying independent citizenship to its poorest residents.

To the extent that Castells was persuasive, the researcher had to consider the constraints that operating in this system of dependencies might have on residential associations in the favelas. In Castells' view, idealistic association leaders would be locked into patronage politics on the terms of the patrons. Even should they strive for autonomy from the normal wheeling and dealing of patronage politics (you association leaders control unruly residents and deliver us the vote and you might get some goodies) they would find it difficult to persuade residents at large to invest scarce time and energy in alternative forms of collective action. Further, when they challenged the limits of the system, first by the sheer volume of their demands for urban services and land rights, and then by demanding recognition of new forms of engagement by shanty-town residents, they would risk failure on all counts: local government neither could, nor would deliver. In turn, the associations would be unable to deliver any of

---

13. Manuel Castells, *The City and the Grassroots: A Cross-cultural Theory of Urban Social Movements* (Los Angeles: University of California Press, 1983).
14. Castells, *The City and the Grassroots*, 212.

the urgently needed material benefits residents demanded. Idealistic association leaders would be abandoned as residents they had been able to mobilise from time to time got on with their lives. In Castells' plangent phrases, the associations and the wider movements they represented would become 'urban shadows', their projects for autonomous voice, social justice, and new democratic practices, would be realised only in 'isolated Utopias'.[15]

One favela was chosen for intensive participant observation research to test hopeful claims against Castells' pessimism. This was the favela of Jardim Oratório in Mauá, a city on the periphery of Greater São Paulo. The author became a resident guest in a shed[16] constructed by residents to house a priest and five seminarians of the Redemptorist order who combined live-in pastoral work with their studies, for which they commuted every weekday to São Paulo city. The Redemptorists had been invited in by Catholic *favela* residents, several of whom had been leaders in CEBs in rural areas of Brazil. Three years prior to the author's arrival in the community, a residents' association, called the Land Commission, had been established. It was similar in its form, programs and modus operandi to other *favela* residents associations in a network that extended throughout São Paulo and beyond. For the Redemptorists who had helped residents set it up, and for Catholic members, the Land Commission was one of several pastoral programs. But its membership extended beyond the Catholic community, and its primary aims were to achieve land tenure, 'urbanisation' and democratic governance for all residents.

In the first four months of fieldwork in 1988, the author attended weekly meetings of the Commission's executive and accompanied its work in between times. The evidence, at the end of fieldwork, seemed to fall on the side of the hopeful rather than the pessimistic perspective on residents' associations. This was no 'isolated Utopia'

---

15. Castells, *The City and the Grassroots*, 327. Note that Castells' full analysis of failed urban movements, including squatters' movements is more subtle than it appears in this outline. Having failed, either by attempting too much (Utopia) or too little (extension of urban services) they may still help produce 'new historical meaning ... nurturing the embryos of tomorrow's social movements.' 331.
16. 'Shed' is the right word, but unlike many shanties in the *favela* at this time, it had a cement floor and water, electricity and waste connections. It was divided by partitions into seven rooms, including separate kitchen and bathroom.

and it resisted cooptation of the kind predicted by Castells into local patronage politics. Its leaders considered themselves to be part of a wider movement, and met regularly with leaders of other, similar associations, informally and in regional assemblies and training seminars for the popular movements. It appeared to exemplify sustainable local civic democracy at work. Discussions of social justice values and strategy in the weekly executive meetings and the neighbourhood assemblies it organised were exhaustive. The executive meetings, under the watchful eye of its elected chairman, a long-time resident of the *favela*, were at once orderly, procedurally correct, and geared to decision-making on a range of diverse matters. These included moving shanties to widen streets; maintaining a cooperative in which residents could make cement bricks for house-construction; building model houses out of the bricks to replace shanties made of bits of wood and plastic; formulating and presenting infrastructure demands to municipal government; producing and distributing bulletins and notices on matters of concern to the Commission, including forthcoming municipal elections. High among the Commission's concerns was the defence and extension of democracy in the Land Commission itself, in the *favela*, and in the municipality at large.

At the end of the first stint of fieldwork, this *favela* residents' association seemed robust in the face of just the sort of challenges outlined by Castells. The Land Commission had several mutually reinforcing sources of strength that sustained it at the time. Members of the executive of the Commission shared a strong civic culture which was grounded, for several key leaders at least, in the theological vision and practices inculcated in the CEBs[17]. The civic culture was continually translated into practical projects for urbanisation. The Commission won support from residents by its peculiar combination of practical concern and action for piped water, housing and sanitation, on the one hand, and a well-articulated

---

17. The theological vision was that of the Theology of Liberation. See Matthew Clarke *Development and Religion* (Cheltenham: Edward Elgar Publishing, 2011), chapter 5 for a brief and accessible outline. The vision featured the poor, in their struggles for social justice, as the pilgrim people of God, seeking to realise the kingdom of God on earth. A key practice of the CEBs was group reflection on daily life in the light of the stories and messages of the bible–readings from the Book of Life in dialogue with readings from the Book of God.

vision which placed local struggles in an emergent, more just, and democratic Brazil. Finally, this local association was supported by a network, extending well beyond the *favela*, which provided material and discursive support to the Commission.

Research has extended over seven fieldwork visits of varying duration, the last brief visit being in 2011. 'Snapshots' of the *favela* and the Commission on successive visits have been presented elsewhere.[18] Suffice to say here, that the mainly hopeful assessments made in the early years, gave way to more sober, though not overwhelmingly pessimistic, accounts in later years. The Land Commission built on its early achievements, but was unable to maintain the high level of mobilisation of residents required if its vision of more just, deeply democratic urban life, generated by the urban poor, were to have been realised. The reasons for this included factors of negative globalisation identified by Castells.

The case of the Land Commission of Jardim Oratório did not stand alone. Throughout the urban periphery of São Paulo, economic globalisation, including the neo-liberal projects of successive governments, have affected employment chances, especially of poor young males, and created an underclass of competitors for scraps in the informal sector of the economy. Gang violence and crime, especially in the *favelas*, have increased as a result,[19] leading residents to abandon their residential associations when they appeared powerless to do anything about increasing insecurity.[20] At the same time, throughout the 1990s, the will and capacity of agencies responsible for the provision of urban infrastructure diminished, again as a result of neo-liberal policies and the chain of squeezes associated with Brazil's debt problems at the time. Even as the debt

---

18. Rowan Ireland, 'Fragile Synergies for Development: The Case of Jardim Oratório SP Brazil', in *The Poverty of the State: Reconsidering the role of the State in the Struggle against Global Poverty*, edited by Alberto Cimadore, Hartley Dean and Jorge Siqueira (Buenos Aires: CLACSO/CROP, 2005), 241–62.
19. Pedro Jacobi, 'Public and private responses to social exclusion among youth in São Paulo', in *The Annals of the American Academy of Political and Social Science*, 606 (July 2006): 216-230.
20. Compare the effects of violence in favelas of Rio de Janeiro discussed in Marcelo Lopes de Souza, 'Social movements in the face of criminal power: The socio-political fragmentation of space and 'micro-level warlords' as challenges for emancipative urban struggles', in *City* 13/1, (2009), 27-52.

problem has been vanquished in the 2000s, the continuation of the same neo-liberal policies has denied adequate urban infrastructure to the poorest sectors of the population, though Brazil as a whole has become richer and the proportion of the population below the poverty line reduced.[21] This has meant that associations like the Land Commission have been unable to deliver on the infrastructure projects they promised to achieve on the basis of partnerships with local government. And so, the fates of the residential associations become: demise; transformation into mediators in patron-client relations with police, local politicians and gang leaders;[22] or as appearances would have it in the Commission's case, survival as an isolated Utopia, just as Castells predicted.

Add to the political economic story another, about the vicissitudes of the Catholic Church's 'liberationist' projects in the favelas, and we find a further reason why residential associations like the Land Commission have been dying in the big cities of Brazil.[23] As the Church has moved away from the pastoral and community-building programs of the Theology of Liberation era, the associations have lost not only material resources once channelled to them through the Church, but also the energies, community-building, and mobilising capacities formerly fostered in the CEBs.[24] At the same time, there

---

21. For a brief summary of current indicators of continuing inequality evident in favela residents' income levels, educational opportunities, access to public services, and employment, see Maria da Piedade Morais 'Condições de vida e moradia nos assentamentos precários brasileiros' in *IPEA: Desafios do Desenvolvimento* 16/25 (2010): 41.
22. Compare an analysis of how leaders of drug gangs replace associations of residents in Rio de Janeiro, in Enrique Arias and Corinne Rodrigues, 'The Myth of Personal Security: Criminal Gangs, Dispute Resolution, and Identity in Rio de Janeiro's Favelas', in *Latin American Politics and Society* 48/4 (2006): 53-81.
23. Goetz Ottmann, *Lost for Words: Brazilian Liberationism in the 1990s* (Pittsburgh: University of Pittsburgh Press, 2002). The Land Commission in Jardim Oratório, like many another favela residents' association, had decisive input from the 'liberationist' Church from its inception. This came in various forms—first from the central parish in Mauá, then from young priests and seminarians who came (invited by residents) to live in the favela as part of a twelve-year fixed term pastoral project, and finally from Catholic tertiary students and junior academics who, on weekends, came into assist the Commission in its literacy training classes, and to provide technical assistance on publications and urbanisation projects.
24. Manuel Vasquez, *The Brazilian Popular Church and the Crisis of Modernity*

is some evidence that a new generation of favela residents, has lost interest in, or given up on the pursuit of the public, collective goods of urbanisation that drove their parents. For the young of 'the popular classes', poorly educated and unskilled, regular formal sector employment is hard to find. Many of the young seek, nonetheless, to become individual cosmopolitan consumers, pursuing lifestyles and products popularised in global youth culture as best they can, often in the drug trade.[25] They become disaffected from, even foes of the residents' associations. Their elders, reduced to being second-class citizens after decades of urban redevelopment by and for elites, abandon communal commitments in the battle for individual survival. The joint effect of these developments—all but the changing emphases in the Church, results, or at least concomitants of economic, political and cultural globalisation—has been shrinkage, or oftentimes, the disappearance of the *favela* residents' associations.

In the case of the Land Commission, it has been shrinkage. It survives in name, but functionally it is a shadow of what it was a quarter of a century ago. Over time, the effects of negative globalisation on Brazil's political economy in general and its cities in particular, have corroded its alternative urbanisation projects and its support base in Jardim Oratório. However, Castells' bleak pessimism has not been completely vindicated. First, it must be remembered, the Commission flourished for at least a decade under precisely the

---

(Cambridge: Cambridge University Press, 1998) illustrates this moving away, and some of its consequences, in a case study conducted in Rio de Janeiro. Having noted failings and attrition of the CEBs, however, it is important to stress that they have by no means disappeared, nor have the vision and the practices associated with them vanished from the Brazilian Catholic Church. See Madeleine Adriance, *Promised Land: Base Christian Communities and the Struggle for the Amazon* (Albany: State University of New York Press, 1995). Also Jan French, 'A Tale of Two Priests and Two Struggles: Liberation Theology from Dictatorship to Democracy in the Brazilian Northeast', in *The Americas*, 63/3 (2007): 409-443.

25. For an early development of this argument, see Geert Banck, 'Mass Communication and Urban Contest in Brazil: Some Reflections on Lifestyle and Class', in *Bulletin of Latin American Research*, 13/1 (1995): 45-60. For a later elaboration with direct reference to the effect of neo-liberal policies of successive governments in Brazil on civil society and the popular movements, see John Gledhill, 'Citizenship and the Social Geography of Deep Neo-liberalization', in *Anthropolgica*, 47/1 (2005): 81-100, especially 90-93.

conditions predicted to doom it, and during that time much was accomplished. In retrospect it can be seen to have pioneered a new form of participatory democracy at the grassroots—not on its own, of course, but jointly with other associations in the network. That achievement is arguably as important as any of the items of material welfare it achieved for residents. Second, we can now see that the shrinkage of the Commission is not identical to the demise of its vision, projects and modus operandi. In later stints of fieldwork, the author has traced 'graduates' of the Commission in its golden days and found some of them carrying the culture and community-building projects nurtured in Jardim Oratório into local government and social movements operating elsewhere. Observers of other residents' associations in other Brazilian cities have noted the same transfers.[26]

It is worthwhile, then, to inquire into the factors that explain the years of flourishing and the cultural survival of the Commission. It is when we do this that we have to acknowledge the vectors in globalisation that are positive for local struggles. As we have seen, the Commission was formed to address conditions arising from, or exacerbated by various processes of contemporary globalisation, and its own development was eventually stymied by these processes. On the other hand, globalisation processes were integral to its genesis, its years of achievement, and its revitalisation after reverses. Like many another *favela* residents' association, the Commission's story includes the involvement of the Catholic Church. But to put the Church into the story is to point to what might be called positive global vectors in the life of local Church communities and in the Land Commission itself.

In its early years, the Commission received small but invaluable financial assistance which was channelled to it through Catholic Church networks linking it to ecumenical funding agencies in Europe. These agencies endorsed, and indeed came to require, the twin strategies of communitarianism and conscientisation.

---

26. See, for example, Márcia Pereira Leite 'Novas Relações entre Identidade Religiosa e Participação Política no Rio de Janeiro Hoje: O caso do Movimento Popular de Favelas', in *Religião e Espaço Público*, edited by Patricia Birman (São Paulo: Attar Editorial, 2003), 63-95. Also, Marcelo Lopes de Souza, 'Social movements in the face of criminal power', 27-52.

Protestant and Catholic overseas aid NGOs financed personnel and plant for projects proposed by the Commission. For several years, for example, three members of the Commission received minimum salaries out of these funds to support their families so that they could work full time on Commission projects, free of the need to work outside the *favela* (they were known as the *Liberados*). The same funds were used to construct a building which included a workshop for cooperative housing construction, and space for meetings and classes. These internationally-sourced funds, long since dried up, were essential to the Commission in its years of highest achievement. The funds enabled the Commission to undertake projects in the *favela* without having to seek out and then go cap in hand to patrons in local government, thereby risking the disastrous outcomes forecast by Castells. The *Liberados*, as they engaged directly in the projects, became the known and trusted faces of a Commission that was getting things done for residents, for some years at least. Then the flow of international visitors to see, assess, and learn from the work of the Commission boosted morale and fed a sense of the importance of local experiments in Jardim Oratório.

That was but one instance of how global connections and the sense of being part of a movement extending far beyond local and national frontiers lent strength to the local association and helped equip it to counter negative forces of globalisation. The Commission was also sustained by a flow of discursive resources across national boundaries which enabled leaders and members–the Catholics especially, but not exclusively–to identify as part of a global movement for justice and peace. Hymns sung with gusto recalled Oscar Romero of El Salvador and other heroes of the Latin American liberationist struggles. The women of Jardim Oratório were linked by song-lines to the women of Latin America fighting against domestic violence and for justice and new roles for women in their communities. In Sunday sermons and on annual pilgrimages organised by the Commission, the faithful of Jardim Oratório developed their sense of solidarity with those who struggled for racial justice, workers' rights and land rights around Latin America. In turn, the identifications and solidarity with other contemporary and historical struggles provided encouragement and a sense of purpose in their own projects.

In these ways global factors operated to sustain Commission activists in their proactive address to local manifestations of negative globalisation. The case by no means allows dismissal of the charges against contemporary globalisation previously outlined. Factors of economic, political and cultural globalisation have all been involved in the ultimate enfeeblement of the Commission, and other residential associations like it in Brazil. However, the story points to several challenges to the bleak pessimism of Manuel Castells' account of the fate of urban squatters' associations in Latin America. More generally, it suggests we look at contemporary globalisation as a set of contradictory processes with negative and positive effects on communal action for social justice and alternative futures. The case suggests too that there in local community associations we will sometimes find resourceful Davids taking on the Goliaths of negative globalisation. Both these conclusions may be elaborated on the basis of the review of a new class of transnational organisations in the next, concluding section.

Globalisation and Transnational Social Movement Organisations (TSMOs)

Since the 1970s, the sorts of transnational organisations that were involved in the development of the Land Commission of Jardim Oratório have proliferated, and the geographical spread and scope of the projects they undertake has expanded enormously. This section concludes the exploration of the contradictions of globalisation with a review of this development, and profiles a few of the TSMOs that, on the one hand are part and parcel of contemporary globalisation, and on the other provide crucial stimulus and resources to local communal associations struggling for land justice, cultural survival, gender justice, work conditions and remuneration justice. TSMOs are not entirely new on the world scene, and indeed many of them are long-established international aid organisations like Oxfam or World Vision with new functions added–at once to address new problems associated with contemporary globalisation, and to help local organisations working locally to survive under conditions of destructive contemporary globalisation. TSMOs then are those formal organisations, operating transnationally, that have developed in tandem with contemporary capitalism's movement toward 'one big self-regulating market'.[27] They seek to coordinate

---

27. Carl Polanyi, *The Great Transformation: The Political and Economic Origins of our Time* (Boston: Beacon Press, 2001), 70.

and sustain exchanges of information, skills and resources between allies in struggles to contest the destructive effects of global market anarchy and/or to realise social alternatives locally. Countering the 'globalisation from above' that may thwart local action for social justice, TSMOs foster and help sustain 'globalisation from below'.[28]

One distinguishing feature of many TSMOs is their commitment, despite their global scope, to those two central strategies of communitarianism and conscientisation, which, of course, can only be realised locally. Lest we get too starry-eyed, it is sobering to read TSMO directors' self-assessments, and case-studies which suggest that performance sometimes falls short of ideal because organisational headquarters and organisation directors are generally still centred in the global North, rather than the South.[29] However, the growing academic literature on TSMOs, reveals their increasingly important role in sustaining local struggles and forming alliances between local groups experiencing injustices with global sources.[30] Jackie Smith in several publications helps us list the functions of TSMOs.[31]

In addition to those already noted, the functions that TSMOs perform at the local level include helping bring together constituencies, for example, unskilled migrant labourers displaced by globalisation of the labour market, which lack 'natural' ties in their host societies. They help channel discursive, material and political support to groups like the shanty-town dwellers of Brazil who are abandoned by governments locked into a 'race to the bottom' in a neo-liberal world. They 'generate and guide a transnational public

---

28. The two types of globalisation are contrasted in Joe Bandy and Jackie Smith, editors, *Coalitions across Borders: Transnational Protest and the Neoliberal Order* (Lanham, MD: Rowman and Littlefield, 2005).
29. Some of these assessments are referred to in Lesley J Wood, 'Bridging the Chasms: The Case of Peoples Global Action', in: *Coalitions across Borders*, edited by Bandy and Smith, 95-117.
30. For example, Ronaldo Munck, *Globalization and Contestation* (London and New York: Routledge, 2007).
31. Jackie Smith, 'Global Civil Society? Transnational Social Movement Organizations and Social Capital', in *Beyond Tocqueville: Civil Society and the Social Capital Debate in Comparative Perspective*, edited by Bob Edwards, Michael Foley and Mario Diani (Hanover NH: University Press of New England, 2001), 194-206.

discourse and debate around global problems'.[32] Smith and others have documented the important role of TSMOs in mediating relations between local groups and global institutions (including UN bodies) dealing with health, gender and environmental justice. As they mediate, they attempt to democratise the global institutions and gain a hearing for the voices of women and groups generally absent from world forums and deliberative assemblies.

WEDO, The Women's Environment and Development Organization, a global women's advisory group has had some notable success in performing the latter function. Having achieved policy commitments from global institutions on women's rights and social, economic and environmental justice, it has turned to work in collaboration with partners from the global South to implement global policy gains at the national and local levels. Other TSMOs, as the list of some of their key functions in the previous paragraph suggests, have different specialisations of concern and modus operandi. *Earth Action*, for example, has a distinguished record in responding to invitations from community groups to globalise their local struggles against development projects sponsored by governments engaged in the 'race to the bottom' for foreign investment. One continuing project started in response to a request for help from Cambodia's Prey Lang Community Network, a coalition of communities of the Kuy indigenous people (about 200.000) who inhabit the vast Prey Lang forest. This is currently being destroyed by government-approved mining and agro-industrial projects undertaken by transnational corporations[33]. *Earth Action*, working with the Community Network, and in coalition with other TSMOs like *Cultural Survival*, has produced Action Kits about Prey Lang and the Kuy people to distribute to partner organisations and key contacts in 165 countries. With its partners, it has raised money and organised international letter-writing and distribution of information to try to persuade and pressure the Cambodian Government to stop, or at least reduce, the destruction of Prey Lang and its indigenous communities.

WEDO and *Earth Action* are only small components of a global

---

32. Smith, *Global Civil Society?* 196.
33. See 'Global Response Campaign Alert Cambodia', in *Cultural Survival Quarterly*, December 2011.

network of TSMOs which has expanded in numbers[34] and scope of activities, and become increasingly effective in harnessing global opportunities in the service of local action for social justice over the last four decades[35]. They are included here not as success stories, but only to amplify and illustrate further the contradictory processes of globalisation revealed in the case study of the Land Commission of Jardim Oratório. In their different ways, *WEDO* and *Earth Action* point to two things. First, in the calls for help they address, they point to globalisation in its various forms as a major factor or primary source of injustices which local groups are unable to address alone. But the partnerships and mediations forged by these and other TSMOs across great historical, geographical and cultural divides, point to another aspect of globalisation. That is, an aspect facilitated by the compression of space and time which is integral to it: globalisation as the process whereby a myriad of diverse communities come to constitute, in promise and actuality from time to time, a world united in exchanges for justice and peace. The members of the CEBs of Jardim Oratório, activists in the Land Commission, might recognise in that world, momentary signs of the emerging kingdom of God.[36]

---

34. From an estimated 200 in in the 1970s to over 1000 in 2005.
35. It is worth noting that TSMOs themselves are only among the more organised elements in a larger array of global entities including global institutions, transnational coalitions, and global social movements.
36. It is interesting to reflect on parallels between this aspect of contemporary globalisation and the notion of 'socialisation' in Pope John XXIII's encyclical *Mater et Magistra* (1961). Socialisation is there described as 'the multiplication of social relationships, that is, a daily more complex interpenetration of citizens, introducing into their lives and activities many and varied forms of association'. Further reflection on globalisation and socialisation may be informed by Neil J Ormerod and Shane Clifton, *Globalization and the Mission of the Church* (London and New York: Continuum, 2011).

Globalisation and Christian Education: Impacts and Responses

Therese & James D'Orsa

The Changing Context of Christian Education

Educators as explorers in a globalising world
Under the impact of globalisation, humans seem destined to move into a qualitatively new era of human life on this planet—the global era. While some of the elements of this phenomenon can be perceived with a degree of clarity, we simply cannot know with any real certainty how it will impact in the decades ahead. The dilemma for educators is that they must make some assumptions about the nature of the world they are preparing young people to enter. This requires that they be explorers, guides and meaning-makers.[1] A question for exploration is—how are the responsibilities, goals and processes of the Christian educator affected and challenged by the globalising context in which Christian education now occurs?

The focus of this paper is the life-world of young people, the impacts that globalisation is having on the relationships that define that life-world, the way young people experience and make sense of these, and some implications for Christian education. While available current research does not yet address the effects of globalisation on the worldview of young people directly, it does help us assess impacts, frame questions, raise issues and suggest answers.[2]

---

1. This theme is developed in Jim and Therese D'Orsa *Explorers Guides and Meaning Makers: Mission Theology for Catholic Educators* (Mulgrave: John Garratt, 2010).
2. Australian studies include Philip Hughes *Putting Life Together: Findings from Australian Youth Spirituality Research* (Fairfield: The Fairfield Press, 2007); Michael Mason, Andrew Singleton and Ruth Webber *The Spirit of Generation Y:*

The life-world of young people
The relationships that shape the life-world of young people are those with self, family and friends, society, the natural world, the faith community, and in many cases, with God.[3] There are two broad frameworks within which these relationships can be understood— *the secular framework and the faith framework*. These frameworks provide young people with two different sets of 'stories' within which they can make sense of the relationships that define who they are and their purpose in living. These stories stand as theme and counter-theme within our culture. Both are impacted by the effects of globalisation.

Within any culture, as anthropologist Paul Hiebert points out,[4] there is an on going tension between a number of themes and counter-themes with the balance point between them constantly being renegotiated as the "plan for living"[5] that characterises the culture adapts to changes in its physical, social and ideational environments. If this balance point shifts too far towards one pole or the other, then major problems ensue. In Western societies questions about the meaning of life exist in this theme and counter-theme tension. This development has such a long history in the West that it is now an integral element of its history of ideas. Noted Australian theologian John Thornhill points out, for instance, that in the late medieval period in Europe life became unduly sacralised. The reaction to

---

Young People's Spirituality in a Changing Australia (Mulgrave: John Garratt, 2007); Marcellin Flynn and Magdalena Mok *Catholic Schools 2000: A Longitudinal Study of Year 12 Students in Catholic Schools* (Sydney: New South Wales Catholic Education Commission, 2002). American studies include Dean Hoge, William Dinges, Mary Johnson and Juan Gonzales *Young Adult Catholics: Religion in a Culture of Choice* (Notre Dame Indiana: Notre Dame University Press, 2001); Christian Smith with Melinda Lundquist Denton *Soul Searching: The Religious and Spiritual Lives of American Teenagers* (Oxford: Oxford University Press, 2005). United Kingdom studies include David Hay *Something There: The Biology of the Human Spirit* (Philadelphia: Templeton Foundation Press, 2007); *Religion, Education and Adolescents: International Empirical Perspectives* edited by Leslie Francis, Mandy Robbins and John Astley (Cardiff: University of Wales Press, 2005).
3. Hughes, *Putting Life Together*, 35.
4. Paul Hiebert *Transforming Worldviews* (Grand Rapids Michigan: Baker Academic, 2009), 46.
5. Louis Luzbetak *The Gospel and Cultures*, revised edition (Maryknoll NY: 1988), 157.

this exaggerated stance saw the emergence of modernity which eventually produced a pendulum swing towards an exaggerated secularisation.[6] The consequence has been that the contemporary search for meaning is polarised between sacred stories and secular stories[7]. Young people have to make sense of life within these now competing sources of meaning.

Secular stories
A major theme in the secular stories is that life has *no meaning other than the one we humans give it*. Life is lived in the here and now and what happens when we die is at best an open question. Humans are seen as the centre of meaning in the universe. This results in an attitude to life which sociologist Christian Smith describes as 'therapeutic individualism'. Therapeutic individualism defines the individual as the source and standard of authentic moral knowledge and authority, and individual self-expression as the pre-occupying purpose of life. Subjective personal experience is the touchstone of all that is authentic, right and true.

> Therapeutic individualism is not so much a consciously and intentionally held ideology, but rather a taken for granted set of assumptions and commitments about the human self, society and life's purpose that powerfully defines everyday moral and relational codes and boundaries in the contemporary United States.[8]

These secular stories translate into a worldview—a frame of reference unconsciously assumed within which people think, judge and feel.

These secular stories place great emphasis on both the capacity of humans to make meaning and the conditions under which meaning can be legitimately made. Some version of the secular story now

---

6. John Thornhill *Modernity: Christianity's Estranged Child Reconstructed* (Grand Rapids MI: Eerdmans, 2000), 4ff.
7. There is great variety found among both the secular and the sacred stories. 'Secular' and 'sacred' represent broad categories distinguished by whether life is understood to include or exclude a transcendent dimension.
8. Christian Smith with Melinda Lundquist Denton *Soul Searching: The Religious and Spiritual Lives of American Teenagers* (Oxford: Oxford University Press, 2005), 172.

stands behind the academic disciplines which legitimate knowledge in the West, and this is something that Christian education has, in general, dealt with rather inadequately. One consequence of this is that contemporary missiologists now see the *construction of knowledge as an important field for Christian mission*

In the Western search for meaning, secular stories revolve around *the individual*. The relationships that define who we are all focus back on 'me'. As a consequence, the relationships that define human identity *tend to be viewed subjectively*. They are a private matter about which one is free to choose. This opens the way for both radical individualism and forms of humanism based on the golden rule. The relationship of 'me' to the faith community in the secular stories is often one of rejection, but it can also be one of acceptance, as we shall see later.

Of course, the picture is more complex than this. There is an objective game being played out below this subjective picture because the terms of the relationships by which we define who we are, are themselves in constant interaction.

Globalisation—impacts on secular stories
Understood in this way, it is easy to assess some of the impacts that globalisation now has on the formation of human identity. Globalisation challenges our understanding of 'society' and how it works. It does this because it challenges the notion of 'culture' as this has been conceived in the nineteenth and twentieth centuries. Globalisation also raises questions about the accepted notion of the modern state that has been dominant for nearly two centuries. Many societies are now struggling to adapt to their new status as multi-cultural entities with semi-porous borders. This is particularly evident in Europe, but it is also true in many parts of Asia and Africa. Some societies are negotiating these changes better than others.

Globalisation which sees the rapid diffusion of new communication technologies has changed the way the term 'friends' is now understood. Young people live in a world of 'real' and 'virtual' friends. When the new technologies are brought into the home they impact on what is understood as 'normal' in family life.

The impact of globalisation also impacts on how we understand 'creation' and our relationship to it. It seems fairly clear that a new stage of human consciousness is emerging based on two realisations.

The first is that *humans have the capacity to destroy the planet* not as the consequence of a nuclear holocaust—a fear that is receding—but as the consequence of greed and how people use the resources of the planet. The second realisation is that the earth's resources have *a finite limit* and that they cannot be exploited indefinitely without destroying the biosphere of the earth. Human consumption now represents the greatest threat to all living species. These two realisations are reshaping the way in which many young people think about and relate to the natural order.

Globalisation also affects the relationship between the individual and the 'faith community', even within the secular story. In one version of the secular story religion was supposed to fade from view to be replaced by science as the principal means of meaning-making. This was the story as told by secularisation theory. However, the reality is that *religious sensibility is undergoing something of a resurgence in the West*, albeit not necessarily accompanied by regular Church attendance. Secondly, the West's efforts to democratise Muslim countries, coupled with the impact of migration with its accompanying pluralism of cultures and religions, has resulted in its having to accept people's religious beliefs as matters of public concern because Muslim peoples on the whole do not buy into the West's determination that 'religion is purely a private matter'. The consequence is that people now talk of the need for a 'post-secular' public square.

The changes outlined above cumulate to define what cultural anthropologists call 'deep change'—that is change at the deepest dimension of a culture. These changes are all complex, only partially realised, and often difficult to understand. Furthermore, they do not occur independently, but interact in complex ways. The consequence is anxiety, now on a massive scale. This is most obvious when we consider the current international economic scene. One has to have some sympathy for young people endeavouring to put their life-world together in a globalising world with all its accompanying uncertainties.

Faith stories
Faith stories provide an alternative meaning structure to the secular stories and stand as a counter-theme to them. Faith stories hold that

life has a source of meaning additional to what humans can devise, and that that source is God. In these stories the meaning of life is *no longer simply a human construction*. In the Christian stories, for instance, the relationships that define our life-world take on new significance because of the continuing intervention of *a personal God* in human history, and the purpose or mission God has in this intervention. This adds a new dimension to the framework within which we pursue these relationships.[9] In the Christian stories the framework takes particular form in the ethic of 'the reign of God' or the 'kingdom of God', which was the predominant metaphor used by Jesus to describe the goal of his mission.

God's mission and quest for relationship with 'me' is made in the context of God's relationship to the faith community. This adds depth to our understanding of all the relationships by which we define ourselves—to society, to the faith community, to the natural world and to family and friends. Our understanding of these relationships and the ethics which govern them are *no longer purely human constructs*. 'Society' can no longer be considered without also considering matters of social justice and equity since all people under God share a common dignity. The culture of people living in any given society is no longer seen simply as a human construct, because God is at work playing a role behind the scenes, so to speak, in the construction of cultures. 'Creation' has to be seen not only in the light of the biblical mandate granting humans governance over it, but also within the balancing biblical mandate which gives humans stewardship over creation as given in the two creation stories in Genesis. 'Family and friends' takes on added significance in the Christian world view which sees the family as the centre from which faith springs. The 'faith community' now plays a central role in taking forward the mission of Jesus in terms of proclaiming his teaching, continuing his mission by sustaining the life of the community though the faith development of its members, and taking practical action to make the kingdom of God present in time. These are some of the implications of believing in the personal God who reveals God's intentions in Jesus. The relationship between *God, incarnate in Jesus, and 'me'* becomes the central axis in understanding our life-world.

---

9. Hughes calls this the 'spiritual' dimension. He develops this concept in establishing the framework within which he analyses the results of the *Generation Y Study*, Hughes, *Putting Life Together*, 30–31.

Living with no story—the situation of young people
While faith stories and secular stories stand as theme and counter-theme in our culture, many young people are caught living between these stories. They commonly construct a belief system of their own choosing to 'fill in the blanks' when it comes to making sense of life. Sociologist Christian Smith traced this development among young people in America in the *National Study of Youth and Religion* (which was been partly replicated in Australia as the *Generation Y Study*).[10] He names the form of religion he commonly encountered among teenagers in America as Moral Therapeutic Deism[11] and identifies its five principal tenets as:

> 1. A God exists who created and orders the world and watches over human life on earth.
> 2. God wants people to be good, nice, and fair to each other, as taught in the Bible and by most world religions.
> 3. The central goal in life is to be happy and to feel good about oneself.
> 4. God does not need to be particularly involved in one's life except when God is needed to resolve a problem.
> 5. Good people go to heaven when they die.

As a popular religion, this faith is 'moral' because it inculcates a moralistic approach to life—'Good moral people live good and happy lives'. It is 'therapeutic' because it is about feeling good, happy, secure and at peace—'Religion is about obtaining subjective well-being'.[12] Finally it is 'deism' because it is predicated on an *impersonal conception of God* with no expectation that one lives in an inter-subjective relationship with God. The result is a DIY (do it yourself) hybrid of the secular and sacred stories which is a parasitic form of Christian faith.

Globalisation—new directions for hope
Globalisation, in changing human consciousness, gives rise to new forms of human aspiration. As people of faith Christians are

---

10. The *Generation Y Study* is reported by both Hughes, *Putting Life Together,* and Michael Mason, Andrew Singleton and Ruth Webber *The Spirit of Generation Y.*
11. Christian Smith with Melinda Lundquist Denton, *Soul Searching* 162-163.
12. Christian Smith with Melinda Lundquist Denton, *Soul Searching* 164.

confident that God's Spirit is at work in this development, even while acknowledging that the task of discerning how this is so, what it means, and what it calls us to, is far from simple. Discernment is particularly so as these aspirations have yet to be clearly articulated. This is the new context faced by educators in dealing with young people. Both teachers and the young people they teach are now caught in a difficult position. Defining who you are in a context that is fluid and in which competing narratives act as *sources of meaning* is not easy. Offering answers to questions young people are not asking in this new context is unhelpful.

In summary then, we have argued that understanding the context in which we work is a pressing issue in Christian education. Theology must be re-contextualised to be meaningful.[13] The life-world framework outlined above provides a useful way of understanding *why the context of Christian education is changing* and of explaining some of the outcomes we are observing among young people. This is one side of the coin. The other is understanding *the processes by which people make meaning in their lives* so that educators can better match educational efforts to this understanding. In the sections that follow we seek to address this issue by exploring how people make meaning in their lives and drawing out some immediate implications for the process or 'how' of Christian education in a globalising world.

Meaning-Making in a Globalising World

Christian education as meaning-making

Christian educators have a responsibility to understand the processes by which young people make sense of their world and the challenges posed by their need to situate themselves within that world. In this sense *Christian education is essentially about meaning-making.* We make sense of our experiences, consciously or unconsciously, by accessing *three public worldviews*. These three public worldviews are the worldview of our culture, the worldview of the age in which we live, and the worldview of our faith community. We explore these briefly to make sense of what follows.

---

13. This point in well made in Stephen Bevans and Roger Schroeder *Constants in Context* (Maryknoll NY: Orbis, 2004). See also Stephen Bevans *An Introduction to Theology in Global Perspective* (Maryknoll NY: Orbis: 2009).

Worldview of Culture
All societies have a more or less successful plan for living together matched to the physical, social and ideational environments in which people find themselves living.[14] Underpinning this plan is a worldview—a framework that enables people to think, judge, and act in a way that is so taken-for-granted that it is rarely examined. This is the cultural worldview. In the West the driving force in its development has been the value placed on *excellence in intellectual enquiry*. Such enquiry has been pursued within a number of different paradigms—scientific, philosophical, historical, literary, and theological. The dominance of the scientific paradigm in the modern period has given rise to knowledge systems, technology systems and, based on these, the complex social systems (political, economic, health, social welfare *etcetera*) that characterise Western societies. It is now impossible to function in Western cultures without the knowledge and skills needed to operate effectively within these systems, so in our schools the public curriculum seeks to ensure students develop these capacities. This makes education not only a *social right* (because without it one simply could not participate in society), but also *a social necessity* (sustaining the systems themselves). As societies have become more complex, the cultural worldview continually adapts.

Worldview of our age
The worldview of an age refers to the framework that underpins the driving human aspirations of a particular era. These aspirations come to be shared across many cultures. The worldview of modernity has been a dominant shaper of cultures in the West for nearly two centuries now. In this respect ours is *a bifurcated age*, with cultures drawing elements from the worldview of modernity (for example criticism of religious institutions), but also incorporating aspects of the post-modern critique (suspicion of all institutions and their claims to power).

Worldview of faith
This worldview is specific to faith communities or groups of such communities. A shared feature in this worldview is the belief that *life has a transcendent dimension*. Our particular interest is the

---

14. Louis Luzbetak *The Church and Cultures* (Maryknoll NY: Orbis, 1988), 156.

worldview of Christian faith which is conveyed in the Christian story as discussed above.

These three public worldviews do not act as independent sources when it comes to making-meaning, because they are *inter-related sources of meaning*. A moment's reflection indicates that each influences the development of the others.

What is a worldview?
Following noted missiologist and cultural anthropologist, Paul Hiebert,[15] we make three points about the worldview concept that highlight why it is so important in meaning–making and therefore in Religious Education:

- *a worldview has three elements—it embraces understandings, feelings and values*. A worldview is more than just a coherent set of ideas—which was an earlier understanding of worldview.
- *worldviews underpin commitments and sustain effort.*

Worldviews are sources of energy to be tapped. Cultures would not survive very long without the commitment of people to stick with the plan for living that is embedded in them. Religious faiths would command little attention without the commitment people have to what they believe. The aspirations which drive an age, for example for freedom or peace, depend on commitments, what people are prepared to do to achieve them.

- *worldviews rest or fall on axioms and assumptions.*

All worldviews involve an act of faith since they are built on assumptions which are taken to be axiomatic and are therefore held to be beyond argument. For instance, the sacred stories mentioned earlier hold that life has a *transcendent dimension*. The worldview of science stands or falls on the axiom that *the world is intelligible*, although science cannot demonstrate this.

---

15. Paul Hiebert *Transforming Worldviews: An Anthropological Understanding of How People Change* (Grand Rapids Michigan: Baker Academic, 2008), 25.

Public worldviews as traditions of meaning
When it comes to making sense of the world and our experience in it, we do so by making reference to *all three worldviews* outlined above. All have something to offer that is important. In hermeneutics these sources of meaning are sometimes referred to as *traditions of meaning*. That is, they provide *coherent cognitive frames of reference* which we utilise in putting together *a personal worldview*.

We all make sense of life from within our personal worldview whether we are aware of it or not. One simple entry point in exploring our personal worldview is to ask the question—'what am I really committed to?' Standing behind the answer to that question is *the cognitive, affective and evaluative framework* a person uses in making sense of, and negotiating, his or her immediate life-world.

The immediate problem posed by globalisation is that it impacts on all three public worldviews so that young people find themselves trying to formulate their personal worldview drawing on *frameworks that have become partly destabilised*. This is the present context of Christian education. An important task in Christian education is therefore to help young learn about:

- *public worldviews and the ways in which they interact* so that they can understand both their strengths and limits
- the *significance of these worldviews as* sources of meaning in forming *a personal worldview* oriented to the Gospel.

How people make sense of their experiences[16]
People make sense of their experiences by reference to the major worldviews with currency in their society. The exact form these have for individuals is *mediated by the communities within which they grow up and are educated*. When it comes to making sense of experience humans follow a pattern. When we study a novel, for instance, we usually look at incidents in it in the light of the whole story. The significance of particular incidents comes into focus in the context

---

16. The work of Shaun Gallagher *Hermeneutics and Education* (Albany: State University of New York Press, 1992), 149–158 is acknowledged as important source material in the discussion which follows.

of the whole. While we understand the whole in terms of the parts, we also understand the parts in terms of the whole. We use this same process in making sense of life. We come to understand things in an *iterative process* in which we understand parts in terms of wholes, which, in turn, leads us to revise our understanding of the wholes.

The problem with this perspective is that it does not recognize *the pre-understandings that we actually bring to the task of understanding what an event means*. For instance, we rarely read a novel from a neutral position. We read it against *the background of our life experience*, whether we realise this or not. Making sense of, or interpreting, events most commonly begins *at the sub-conscious level*, rather than at the conscious level. Before we begin to make sense of an event, we already have a range of pre-understandings that shape how we 'read' it. These bias our interpretation. Our pre-understandings, in turn, depend on *traditions of meaning* that are embedded in our personal worldview.

Most people make sense of *things primarily in terms of the worldview of culture*, as this is their most immediately accessible frame of reference. Culture provides a *de facto* basis for interpreting things.

However, when we interpret an 'event' and act on our understanding of it, we produce some form of reaction in others or ourselves that provides us with feedback about the worth of our interpretation. When the reaction is positive we may think to ourselves: 'I got it right! I have interpreted the situation correctly'. However, if the reaction is negative, it may well cause us *to question the frame of reference* that we have used to make sense of the event. The great value of traditions of meaning is that we accept them *as reliable frames of reference* because they have been tested in human experience. We subconsciously depend on them as reliable frames of reference and rarely review them. However, as we consciously engage in the process of *meaning-making*, we become aware of the dependence we have on traditions of meaning and the biases they contain.[17]

---

17. Moderate hermeneutics is associated with Gadamer who has been influential in shaping our perceptions on mission education. See Hans-Georg Gadamer, *Truth and Method*, second revised edition, revised translation by Joel Weinsheimer and Donald Marshall (New York: Crossroad Press, 1989).

The normal meaning–making sequence flows from traditions of meaning to interpretation to event. When this proves unproblematic it reinforces our acceptance of the traditions of meaning on which our personal worldview depends. However, once we begin to have doubts about our interpretation because of the consequences which follow, then we are forced to *re-examine the frameworks that stand behind our meaning-making, and which we take more or less for granted*. This becomes especially challenging when they are undergoing significant re-development or when they are at variance with each other in suggesting how to make sense of something.

Meaning-making and Christian education
A significant challenge in Christian education today is knowing how to help young people understand and utilise effectively the sources of meaning available to them in making sense of their life-world. Young people often find themselves in a conflicted position when they perceive that the worldview of faith is at variance with the worldview of culture or the worldview of their age. However, lacking the perspectives and tools needed to resolve such clashes, they simply choose one worldview over the other, or cobble together a composite framework, leaving underlying tensions unresolved. Both religion and science are currently falling victim to this trend.[18] The result is that many young people are accepting neither the sacred story nor the secular story.[19]

Shaping Educational Responses in the Emerging Global Context

Globalisation affects how people make sense of their world because it impacts on the frameworks and processes which people use in meaning-making. We conclude by looking at three ways in which this is the case, and name areas of necessary response for the Christian educator.

---

18. Young people in the present era are more aware of the limitations of science and suspicious of its claims than was the case in the modern era with its believe in 'progress' delivered through science. Science is often viewed as a two-edged sword. This is a post-modern phenomenon.
19. One interpretation of the works of Hughes, *Putting Life Together,* and Christian Smith with Melinda Lundquist Denton *Soul Searching,* is that sixty per cent of contemporary teenagers fall into this category.

Developing an historical consciousness in young people
Globalisation has resulted from developments in technology which make communications possible at unprecedented rates. Having access to these technologies is now critical to the welfare and wellbeing of citizens. This development is bringing about fundamental cultural changes. The worldview of the culture has to evolve to make such changes possible. This means that *most people's primary frame of reference in meaning-making is unstable.*

Due to the communications revolution, much of what now happens in the world can be experienced in real time, so that human life is experienced as compressed in both time and space. Furthermore, the availability of instant information means that life for many is lived in the present with little thought for the future. People are ignorant of what has been learned from the past which is often viewed as irrelevant. The result is that young people become disengaged from the essential narratives through which both culture and faith are transmitted. This has a major impact on their capacity to form the coherent personal worldview needed to make sense of their life-world. Since worldviews are conveyed as stories, the development of historical consciousness is critical to meaning-making. *Lack of historical consciousness is both problematic and challenging for Christian educators since Christianity holds that God is revealed to us in and through our history.*

Responding positively to pluralism
Globalisation results in other mega-phenomena that contribute very significantly to the situation of deep change. With the unprecedented movement of people across the world, globalisation results in previously unimaginable pluralism *embracing cultures, religions and ideologies.* The consequence is that young people are confronted with a wide range of options. *Christian education must, therefore, be responsive to this pluralism.*

The pluralised nature of societies opens up in a new and stark way the whole area of knowledge construction and how we humans seek truth. It forces us to consider the heart of the educational process—*the pursuit of truth and meaningful knowledge.* In Western educational tradition the modern construction of knowledge has been taken as a given. The post-modern critique challenges this situation. Christian educators need to be aware of the nature of this challenge and the possibilities it opens up. This is a key element in the re-contextualisation of Christian education. It becomes imperative to understand the various ways in which people in different cultures construct knowledge, so that the Western model is seen in context, so that young people are not trapped in the ethnocentric 'West is best' stance which has been so destructive in its effects.

Preparing young people to contribute in the post-secular public square
The pluralised nature of many societies produced by globalisation is giving rise to a new concept of secularisation. Instead of the notion of 'public square' as a *social space free from religion*, it is now widely realized that such an approach, with its roots in Western history, is unhelpful in the contemporary world for a number of reasons. Not least of these is dealing positively with the issues important to people of religious faith, who constitute such a large percentage of humanity. The "post-secular" public square reflects a new configuration of the three public worldviews people access in making sense of life. Its emergence has the potential to enhance human aspiration in a globalised world. It creates a social space in which people of different cultures, faiths, and ideologies can meet in dialogue in such a way that they can learn from each other, and work together to build a better society. *An important goal for Christian education therefore lies in developing the understandings, dispositions and skills needed to function as Christian citizens in this new public square.*

Conclusion

The experience of educating in a social situation which is demanding, complex and at times confusing, generates both soul-searching and creativity. Christian educators now find themselves re-examining the fundamental beliefs and values that underpin their commitment to teaching. This is a by-product of self-reflection which consciously explores the sources they call on in making sense of the world. As we have argued elsewhere, to be effective in their role, Christian educators need to develop the capacity to be self-reflective and to theologise—'do' theology rather than simply learning theology. *'Doing theology' means bringing the worldviews of faith, culture and the age into relationship when creating meaning, recognising that each has an important contribution to make.* In this context, support for and ongoing education of Christian teachers are now serious obligations placed on any Christian community which sponsors the education of the young. An attitude of 'business as usual' simply betrays the nature of this obligation in a globalising world.

Global Mission:
Consequences for the Marginalised

Robyn Reynolds

Introduction

Today we are in an age of religious as well as economic and technological globalisation. Peoples of the world are becoming more aware that all cultures and religions can proclaim and witness to the betterment of humanity and can in fact be manifestations of God's presence in the world. Increasingly it is acknowledged that universally there are many shared beliefs and hopes; a religious as well as cultural pluralism is being recognized and valued. Global mission offers new opportunities for more sustained inter-religious and inter-cultural dialogue.

In earlier centuries the modern missionary movement was generally associated with expansion, conquest and colonisation; mission theology and practice was Eurocentric and Western. But with the emergence and spread of twentieth century post-colonialism, European Christianity and culture lost its place of prominence and power.

In the twenty first century, we see the emergence of new realities, different democracies. Along with development however, globalisation has brought devastation and division, whether it be economic, cultural, political, environmental, social or religious.

It is important to note that advances in global travel and communication, have enabled enthusiastic, sometimes extremely enthusiastic modern day missionaries to embark upon short term mission enterprises, sometimes with severe consequences (as seen for example in 2007, when the Korean Presbyterian missionaries were kidnapped by the Taliban in Afghanistan).

Global mission is about the reconciliation of peoples. Its context is alongside the marginalised, the poor of the earth, and the earth itself; its motivation is discipleship and service. Furthermore, authentic global mission today means prophetic witness, as it involves a radical response to *Missio Dei*, which is the transforming work of God in the world.

Missiologist Thomas Grenham promotes a language of empowerment rather than imposition. 'There is a necessity, given the current global interdependence of cultures, for an interreligious and intercultural relationality that seeks boundless life for everyone, especially for those who have yet to discover life-giving relationships within social structures.'[1]

The focus of my paper is to underline the fact that in the discourse on global mission, the voice of indigenous peoples, women, as well as other marginalised groups, requires and demands inclusion.

Hearing indigenous peoples

> There was a rich man who was dressed in purple and fine linen and lived in luxury every day. At his gate was laid a beggar named Lazarus, covered with sores, and longing to eat what fell from the rich man's table. Luke 16:19–21

Why is it that we continue to address so inadequately the cries of the poor and in particular of the country's indigenous peoples? Is there some perceived benefit in doing so? What is it we are resisting? Of what are we suspicious?

When Pope John Paul II addressed Aboriginal Australians in 1986 in Alice Springs, he spoke of the church in Australia, saying that it 'will not be fully the Church Jesus wants her to be until you have made your contribution to her life and until that contribution has been joyfully received by others.'[2] John Paul's words continue to ring true, awaiting realisation. Do we believe that the voice of the poor might be redemptive, making global mission a mutual endeavour for the benefit of all?

---

1. Thomas Grenham, *The Unknown God: Religious and Theological Inculturation* (Oxford: Peter Lang, 2005), 295.
2. Pope John Paul 11, *The Pope in Australia: Collected Homilies and Talks* (Sydney: St Paul's Publications), 1986.

The lived reality as Aboriginal Australians know, is grim, the outlook dismal. For most Aboriginal groups and communities the reality reflects a decline rather than improvement in the people's well-being. The likelihood of educational and employment options for indigenous Australians is uncertain at best. For very many Aboriginal males a prison term is likely.[3] Aboriginal women, men and children are familiar with discrimination, racism, domestic violence, serious health issues, life-long poverty and neglect; it is rare not to fear or expect an early death for oneself and one's family; furthermore it is uncommon not to feel one's cultural identity being drained away, one's land stolen and degraded, one's spirituality and law belittled and devalued.

These are some of the 'sores' that cover the bodies and spirits of countless Australian Aboriginals today. Lazarus is right before us if we dare look. In a paper discussing Aboriginal perspectives on Christian belief and practice, well known Aboriginal leader, Pat Dodson has written that 'there was no dialogue, never any real consideration of being Aboriginal people. There was a remaking and remoulding and restructuring and a reorienting of our society without any negotiation with us.'[4] Tragically, to Australia's shame, eyes, ears and hearts too often stay closed. Or even with some awareness and concern, there remains the reluctance to intentionally engage with Aboriginal people co-operatively and respectfully.

Where the Racial Discrimination Act has been suspended or 'modified' to enable Aboriginal welfare payments to be tied to a child's school attendance, it is discriminatory and would never be implemented amongst other groups. No proper consultation has been done with Aboriginal leaders and communities and as Jesuit scholar and social justice advocate, Frank Brennan sj has recognized, this docking of moneys is a 'racially targeted' one.[5]

---

3. Aboriginal and Torres Strait Islander people make up 26 per cent of the prison population, while being only two and a half per cent of the total population and in the Northern Territory, Aboriginal and Torres Strait Islander people form 80.6 per cent of the prison population (*Building Bridges, not Walls: Prisons and the Justice System*, Australian Bishops Social Justice Statement. Australian Catholic Bishops Conference, 2011), 5.
4. Pat Dodson, 'Leaving Culture at the Door: Aboriginal Perspectives on Christian Belief and Practice', in *Pacifica*, 19/3 (2006), 256.
5. Frank Brennan SJ, 'Labor's Intervention on Steroids', in *Eureka Street*, 21

The international award winning Australian film 'Samson and Delilah', with Aboriginal producer, director and actors, was a film depicting experiences of suffering, struggle and alienation. The cross was a significant and recurring image in this remarkable and profound film which carried stories of loyalty and forgiveness, a film wrapped in the mystery of deep pain and love. Consequences of globalisation include displacement and urbanization where desert Aboriginal people such as those seen in 'Samson and Delilah' sometimes have no choice but to move into the fringe camps of Alice Springs for survival.

At this point in our reflection, I think it is important to emphasise the risk of talking too easily of 'the victims', 'the sufferers', even of 'the 'marginalised'. Stereotypes are always dangerous, denying the dignity and distinctiveness of persons and the complexity of individual and communal contexts and experiences. Every person, especially those who have been denied a voice, has a story to be told and heard.

Australian 'missions' to the indigenous people were often complicit in the belittling or dismissal (if not eradication) of traditional spirituality, along with the removal of peoples and groups from their own lands. Aboriginal people tell us often that along with the earth, they have been here since the Dreamtime. It is not surprising Aboriginal persons today ponder the similarities between colonisation and globalisation and how their positions have changed so little. In the new world order of global consumerist capitalism, the beneficiaries are certainly not the indigenous poor.

Because of globalisation, indigenous groups sometimes face almost insurmountable socio-economic challenges: subsistence local economies are crushed by larger scale industries and multinational corporations, as well as by Government bodies which are often deceptive, greedy and corrupt. For example some Aboriginal communities leasing land to the Commonwealth Government discover that the rent they receive is from money paid by the mining Companies into the Aboriginal Benefits Account, which in fact is meant to provide support and services for Aboriginal communities. If mission is to be transforming, Christian individuals and groups need to stand alongside disadvantaged Aboriginal groups and to find

---

November, 2011, http://www.eurekastreet.com.au/article.aspx?aeid=29139#.UowuKeLWGZQ

better ways to work in partnership for more transparent, just and holistic outcomes.

Despite the almost unsurmountable setbacks, and sometimes near overwhelming difficulties, indigenous Christians continue to provide inspiration and leadership. Missiologists such as Robert Schreiter have recognised that as the Christian church becomes increasingly a church of the poor, the worldwide movement of Christianity 'is running counter to the globalising movements of the world economic system'.[6] In the postcolonial era, formerly colonized peoples are often playing a significant role in the unfolding of the Christian story. Many former 'mission' churches have become the new evangelizers. Small Christian Communities in South Africa, for example, breathed new life and energy into the meaning of 'church'; in Latin America, Basic Christian Communities manifested their own radical ways of living and spreading the Gospel message; in remote and urban Aboriginal communities in Australia, groups have exercised and continue to exercise creative leadership.

The Aboriginal Catholic Ministry (ACM) in Melbourne is one such group. With the Education Department's new National Curriculum to be implemented in 2012, ACM leaders have recognized a need to initiate and provide programs to assist teachers in Catholic schools in the delivery of programs relating to Aboriginal life and culture. The Aboriginal leaders see this very much as 'mission in action', a work of and for the Australian church. ACM co-ordinator and Aboriginal leader, Vicki Walker has said that social justice needs to be about 'a practical way of sharing resources, for example in the areas of employment for Aboriginal people, education, and health . . . I think we need to look at a more holistic picture when it comes to changes in the relationship between Aboriginal people and the church.'[7]

Engaging in mission means addressing the huge wrongs and inequalities in our nation, and moving together to build God's reign of compassion for the whole human family, including in particular, its indigenous peoples.

---

6. Robert J Schreiter 'Reconciliation as a Model of Mission', in *Landmark Essays in Mission and World Christianity,* edited by Robert L Gallagher and Paul Hertig (Maryknoll NY: Orbis Books, 2009), 65.
7. Vicki Walker, 'Vignette', in *Pacifica,* 19/3 (2006): 264.

The Voice of Women

> There was a widow in that same town who kept coming to him and pleading for her rights. Luke 18:3

This parable is about the importance of constancy and trust in praying. An imaginative reading of the parable might envision the widow as God, who keeps coming, pleading for her rights: 'Help me against my opponents!' God is on the side of the oppressed, the side of those whose rights are being denied or ignored, on the side of women whose voices are being shut out. God is in solidarity with those who cry out for justice. Women (and also men who are being disenfranchised) can take comfort—and continue to cry out with passion and hope.

Religious and cultural encounters have been happening over the centuries as the Gospel message has been passed on by women. In fact, according to historian Dana Robert, the growth of Christianity in the two-thirds world today should be analysed as a woman's movement: 'When we ask the question of why the world church seems to be predominantly female, we are not just making a sociological observation. We are actually raising the profoundly important issue of gender-based approaches to mission.'[8] One such approach and an example of a woman's voice that was heard (though too soon tragically silenced) was Annalena Tonelli. The impact of her message and her life continues to resound.

In 1969 Annalena, as a young Italian Catholic, went to teach in Kenya to work with Somalian Muslim refugees. On seeing the extent of tuberculosis, Anna returned to Europe to study tropical medicine, after which time she spent the next thirty-three years in Africa. In 1984 she was arrested and expelled for criticising persecution against a group of desert nomads. Annalena worked constantly to improve the health of women and girls; her opposition to female genital mutilation for example, was widely recognized. Annalena worked in the background but never in isolation, staying always in partnership with and in service to Muslim leaders and midwives. She broke through religious, ecclesial, cultural, gender and political boundaries

---

8. Dana Robert, *Christian Mission: How Christianity became a World Religion* (West Sussex, United Kingdom: Wiley-Blackwell, 2009), 61.

with the words and actions of love. Annalena's vision was global, her particular mission was local. She told authorities she defended the people for the sake of Jesus Christ, proclaiming *ut unum sint* (that all may be one) as the deepest yearning of her soul.[9] Annalena was shot twice in the head as she worked in the hospital. Not surprisingly, for Muslim and Christian, she remains an inspiration to this day. For those with whom she journeyed, her understanding and living out of mission certainly had profound consequences. German theologian, Katja Heidermanns identifies perspectives that transcend geographical boundaries, Annalena's legacy surely. Heidermanns believes the feminist challenge is 'to understand mission in a way that opens up liberating spaces by enabling people to recognize our global interdependence and responsibility for our common past and present'.[10]

Three years before Annalena's death, the Parliament of the World's Religions produced a 'Declaration Towards a Global Ethic'. It incorporated a commitment to equality between women and men, condemned all forms of patriarchy, exploitation of women and children, insisting that 'there is no authentic humaneness without a living together in partnership'.[11]

As we asked earlier in relation to indigenous peoples, we can ask similar questions in reference to women: of what are we afraid or why are we reluctant in addressing the words, the dreams, the challenges that women pose?

Some argue that aspects of global mission today could be seen as another form of patriarchy, certainly in view of definitions given by such scholars as Sandra Schneiders who sees a patriarchal system as 'fundamentally a masculine power structure in which all relationships are understood in terms of superiority and inferiority and social cohesion is assured by the exercise of dominative power'.[12] As it is,

---

9. 'The Only Thing That Counts', in *World Mission Magazine*, 15/11 (December 2003), http://www.world mission.ph/December03/nnalena%20Tonelli.htm
10. Katja Heidemann, 'Missiology of risk: Explorations in Mission Theology from a German Feminist Perspective', in *International Review of Mission*, 93/368 (January 2004): 111.
11. Hans Kung, *A Global Ethic: The Declaration Towards a Global Ethic*, edited by Hans Kung and Karl-Josef Kuschel (London: SCM Press, 1993), 33.
12. Sandra Schneiders, *Women and the World* (New York: Paulist Press, 1986), 13.

despite important changes that the women's movement has brought at different levels, today many women still find that they are locked into systems of discrimination and cycles of poverty which prevent access to professional training as well as blocking opportunities for human advancement and growth. Abraham dreams of a church, serving mission, which is 'a community characterized by egalitarian relationships in which the excluded and marginalised are brought into the circle of communal care'.[13]

Patricia Madigan's research recognises similar needs and problems. Madigan investigated the relationships between gender, religion, economics and politics. She concludes that with the 'social and cultural shifts that have accompanied the globalization process, religions have tended to turn inwards to concentrate on shoring up their own structures of patriarchal power instead of showing concern for those who are suffering most from the ensuing 'maldevelopment'—the poor, most of whom are women'.

In 'developing' countries women make up the majority of the world's poor; of those who are illiterate in the world, two-thirds are women; women do more than fifty per cent of the world's work but receive only ten per cent of the income[14] and, furthermore, even in developed countries, one in every three women experiences violence.

Unfortunately some groups serving the needs and interests of globalisation have not furthered the rights or conditions of women, despite the increasing interest and respect for the diversity of religious and cultural traditions that grew in the 70s and 80s. In the Australian political debates currently surrounding the asylum seekers for example, there is little serious attention given to the situation of women. Reasons for on or off shore processing are unashamedly political and financial, not greatly if at all influenced or informed by the conditions, rights, and voices of women.

My understanding, which brings a feminist or inclusive perspective on global mission, involves addressing abuses of kyriarchal power which also incorporate the abuses which both women and men inflict upon the earth and the whole planetary

---

13. Susan Abraham, *Frontiers in Catholic Feminist Theology* (Minneapolis: Fortress Press, 2009), 204.
14. Patricia Madigan, *Women and Fundamentalism in Islam and Catholicism: Negotiating Modernity in a Globalized Word* (Oxford: Peter Lang, 2011), 210.

system.¹⁵ The invitation and need for witness to God's peace, love and justice are everywhere, amongst children, women and men and in all places. If global mission is to be credible and effective in today's context, along with attentiveness to cosmological and environmental concerns, it needs to address issues of class, race and gender.

According to Linda Woodhead 'If anyone still doubts the importance of the topic of women and religion, it should be enough to point out that the religions which are going to survive and flourish in a new millennium will be those that are most successful in attracting women and providing the social spaces for the articulation of their fears and desires in a rapidly changing world.'¹⁶

Global mission in the twenty first century will either be insular and self-serving, or it will be fluid, engaging and life-giving. The contribution – or the exclusion of the voice and experience of women will largely determine the outcome.

Who is My Neighbour?

> A Samaritan, who was travelling that way, came upon the man, and when he saw him, his heart was filled with pity. Luke 10:33

Perceiving global mission today is still often reduced to a western colonial context, rather than being understood as a complex inter-religious, inter-cultural endeavour. The desire to share Christian faith, to promote the flourishing of the human family and to further God's reign throughout the earth and in all of creation, means crossing cultures and religions to bring this about, remembering the familiar theme 'no world peace without religious peace'.

Susan Smith has shown how other religions (and we could add other persons like the Good Samaritan in Jesus' parable) can mediate God's salvation. She suggests that 'papal teaching on the

---

15. In a narrow sense *feminist theology* can be seen to address issues to do with patriarchy and the exclusion of women, with *womanist theology* moving beyond gender divides and considering matters dealing with race, and class oppression as well. I tend to use the term 'inclusive' to best describe my own position.
16. Linda Woodhead, 'Women and Religion', in *Religion in the Modern World*. edited by Linda Woodhead (London: Routledge, 2002), 352.

universality of the Spirit's presence has implications for missiology and for ecclesiology . . . It invests all of human and cosmic history with religious significance, thereby subverting the sacred/secular dichotomy.'[17]

Who is my neighbour? The question posed by the lawyer in the gospel remains all-important in our day. The life of others as well as our own survival and growth, lies in the answer we give. Our companions on life's journey, especially the marginalised, desperately await our response: a response made out of love, a Christ-like response, to be God's Heart on earth.

African scholar, Musimbi Kanyoro, believes that indigenous persons, those who are women, those born of lower caste, or persons under eighteen years of age, will probably be poor. She writes: 'Poor people lack opportunities to realise their potential. They lack power, influence, voice, and they are extremely vulnerable to sickness, violence and disasters. People who are poor live with a toxic environment, crime, low quality education and are feared by others' where, as Kanyoro recognises, the poor

> stand accused of flaunting the values by which 'decent people' live, while claiming rights to benefits they have not worked for . . . Poor people are often branded as dishonest, lazy, addicted to welfare, capable of fraud, corruption, bribery, vice, drug addiction, alcoholism and substance abuse, criminality, youth hooliganism, theft, mugging, robbery, pick-pocketing, etc.[18]

Along with and arguably because of globalising movements, we see increased social and political upheaval. Certain factors, for example the geographical location of our birth, our gender and race can determine the ways in which globalisation will impact on us. As many people are forced to leave their homelands, the future for themselves and their children is one of uncertainty, discrimination and poverty. The huge increases in aggregate wealth across the world have been distributed in ways that favour some and penalise others.

---

17. Susan Smith, *Women in Mission* (Maryknoll NY: Orbis Books, 2007), 205-210.
18. Mussimbi Kanyoro, 'The Shape of God to Come and the Future of Humanity', in *Concilium* (2004/5): 60.

As the gap between rich and poor continues to widen, Thomas Grenham claims that bridging this gap 'depends upon awakening a global consciousness that each human life is integrally connected to the welfare of all'.[19]

However, to some extent at least, globalisation has anaesthetised us to the deep sufferings of others in our world. It has fed tendencies towards isolationism, protectionism, even racism and has increased social inequality. On the road of corporate and individual greed, consumerism and materialism have been easily and quickly followed.

Maureen O'Connell suggests there is a need to devise 'ethical strategies' that seek to change not only the circumstances faced by the vast majority of humanity, but also the 'oppressive circumstances in which the privileged minority find themselves', since it is this minority which control and are controlled by the dehumanizing systems and structures of globalisation.[20]

In the face of this great divide, to do nothing is an abdication of our moral responsibility. A spirit of humility, vulnerability and receptivity is needed. All of us, including leaders, are challenged to manifest authenticity in relating to others, working towards greater solidarity, not increased uniformity. Rather than remaining comfortable in social exclusion, the invitation is to move towards a genuine hospitality of the heart extending to the whole of creation. Mission will be incomplete, without credibility and ineffective unless it is addressing the cry of the oppressed and of the entire earth.

But here in Australia—as elsewhere—good intentions are not enough. When Aboriginal Australians are stereotyped, belittled, devalued, there is need for urgent and systematic change. When women are being excluded or dehumanised, there is a responsibility to protest, to express outrage and concern and to work for a better reality. When globalisation expands at the cost of the marginalised, the call to actively participate in *Missio Dei* is abundantly clear. The invitation is there, as it was when Jesus put the challenge to the lawyer in the parable. Those abandoned, scorned and penalized by society await ones with the will, the faith and the courage who, like the Good Samaritan, might 'go and do likewise' (Lk 10:37).

---

19. Grenham, *The Unknown God: Religious and Theological Inculturation*, 269.
20. Maureen O'Connell, *Compassion: Loving Our Neighbour in an Age of Globalization* (Maryknoll, NY: Orbis Books, 2009), 194.

The transforming way forward is not one to be 'programmed' as such. It is a work of grace and as Schreiter has discussed, it is a spirituality rather than a strategy that is needed: 'The free, reconciling gift of God's love, which restores a damaged humanity, makes it possible for the victim to love others . . . It is they who become agents of God's reconciliation and it is through them that reconciliation will eventually take place'.[21]

A final comment: Even in such Western democracies as Australia, it is difficult to continue speaking of particular groups, such as Christians, as 'mainstream'. 'Mainstream' groups, lines, classifications are continually shifting and the vulnerable, the forgotten ones, those dismissed or disempowered may be found in all times and places, among people everywhere: 'the poor you will always have with you' said Jesus (Mt 26:11).

However for many, their place is a privileged one where at least some financial and social security exists, some degree of personal and communal well-being is present, and where there is no experience of an on-going struggle for survival. The danger in this case is of being lulled into a sense of complacency, of guilt, helplessness, or a sense of disconnectedness from those in the human family—those parts of our body—wounded or broken.

'Action on behalf of justice and participation in the transformation of the world fully appear to us as a constitutive dimension of the preaching of the Gospel.'[22] Such key texts bring to mind the earlier statement from the Second Vatican Council's *Ad Gentes* document: 'the church is missionary by its very nature'.[23] Ecclesial statements such as these are most relevant, challenging continued reflection in the light of today's world. Mission matters, and has global as well as ecclesial ramifications. Grenham suggests that 'empowerment

---

21. Robert Schreiter, 'Reconciliation as a Model of Mission', in *Landmark Essays in Mission and World Christianity* edited by Robert L Gallagher and Paul Hertig (Maryknoll, NY: Orbis Books, 2009), 69.
22. Synod of Bishops, *Justice in the World*, 1971, No 6, in Joseph Gremillion, *The Gospel of Peace and Justice: Catholic Social Teaching since Pope John* (Maryknoll NY: Orbis, 1976), 514.
23. Vatican ll, *Ad Gentes* (Decree on the Church's Missionary Activity) in *The Documents of Vatican Council II*, edited by Walter M Abbott, SJ (London: Geoffrey Chapman, 1967) paragraph 2.

should be reflected in the way the gospel vision is shaped according to the unique cultural and religious contours of every context. The inclusion of the marginalised, the alienated, and the vulnerable needs to form a significant component of Christian evangelisation everywhere, especially within the visible structure of the church.'[24]

The call is not to deny or avoid the difficulties, but to wrestle with them. This paper calls for increased awareness and compassion. Hearts, as well as minds, need to be activated. The call is also for a renewed solidarity in standing alongside suffering and struggling companions on the journey. What I have hoped to highlight is the need for empathy, for ways to awaken this and to act upon it, an empathy calling to conversion from egocentrism that will guard against the tendency to dismiss or dehumanize others, an empathy that will be habitual and transformative.

Mission today is a globalised one and if Christian mission is to further God's 'reign' on earth, this means authentic engagement especially with the world's poor. For the marginalised, consequences inherent in global mission, are a matter of life or death.

---

24. Grenham, *The Unknown God: Religious and Theological Inculturation*, 260.

Ernst Troeltsch on Christianity in a Globalising World

Wes Campbell

The image of blue planet earth against the dark velvet of the universe is a reminder that we live on one globe. From a more mundane point of view, for several centuries European missionaries and traders challenged the tyranny of distance and travelled the oceans around the globe. In the latter half of the twentieth century, faced with the interlacing of capitalist technocratic, economic power and poverty, recognising the cost of modern technocratic society on the two-thirds of humanity, we learned to speak of the Third World and of 'North and South'. In this present century, though strangely controversial, the warming of the earth and the threat of rising waters focused humanity's concern and care for the planet. In recent years, with the emerging 'green' parties the Occupy movement emerged, pointing to the inequity of wealth and power (one per cent and ninety-nine per cent) even in so-called advanced or 'developed' nations.

The twentieth century commenced with the First World War—particularly experienced in Europe—followed by the Second World War which spread around the globe. Its effects were experienced in the latter half of the century as the Cold War which divided 'East' and 'West' and plunged the whole earth into the danger of a nuclear holocaust and subsequent nuclear winter. In that global setting, the removal of the Berlin Wall and nuclear disarmament talks between the two superpowers generated hopes of a world unified in peace.

Such expectations, however, failed to take account of the impact of the imperial power exercised by the United States, and the growing restiveness among those who experienced its impact. Going to the heart of that imperial power, the terrorist attacks in 2001 brought to the light unresolved complaints, and produced a new shock wave of globalism, in the form of acts of terror. The resulting invasions of Iraq and Afghanistan, on the one hand sought credibility through international forums and alliances, and on the other provoked ongoing acts of resistance and suicide bombing. At the same time, people travel around a globe which has fewer borders (visiting former places which generated fear—China, for example); and those who perpetrate acts of terror also cross those boundaries.

Here we must be careful, as popular use of the language of terror creates a form of 'the other', who dresses and believes differently and is therefore an opponent. However, seen from the viewpoint of those peoples who have experienced, and continue to experience economic oppression and military invasion, *terror* is what they experience at the hands of the United States and other allied powers. A concrete example may be found in the developing use of so-called 'drones'; unmanned aircraft, controlled remotely from the United States as they fly across borders from Somalia to Pakistan—a lethal form of globalisation.

This paper takes up the work of Ernst Troeltsch, a Christian theologian and philosopher of religion, whose work spanned the later decade of the nineteenth century and the first three decades of the twentieth century. Troeltsch attempted to deal with the dramatic relativising experienced in modern European culture. On the one hand, that relativising was produced *internally* by modern scientific thought, including historical research, and producing a fragmentation within European society. And *externally*, Christianity was relativised by its place in global life, along with a number of other world religions. For our present purposes we might say that Troeltsch faced the relativising impact of globalisation. As a consequence, he rejected the absoluteness or superiority of Christianity over against other cultures. Facing the relativism produced by globalisation and then more acutely nihilism, he sought to find a secure footing for Christian faith in a globalised setting among the plurality of cultures.

Perhaps it is anachronistic to be dealing with Troeltsch in this way. I judge that it is helpful to read Troeltsch within this frame in order to explore a self-conscious theological attempt to mark out a place for Christian faith in a time and place when it seemed that Christianity had no future. That he took into his work the profound challenge to Christianity's claim to supremacy and pride of place within the multiplicity of cultures and religions, demonstrates one clear path for Christianity: a refusal to claim to be absolute in such a way that it negates or destroys other world religions and cultures. At the same time, Troeltsch acknowledged that Christian faith was in fact experienced as absolute for the Christian believer, and Christian theology was required to give an account of that existential reality.

This paper explores Ernst Troeltsch's response to the crisis produced for Christian faith by modernity, a modern crisis which we may now name *globalisation*. We will follow that exploration with a brief account of Jürgen Moltmann's response whose work spans the middle of last century to the present and is characterised by the horizon of the coming kingdom of God.

Troeltsch grappled with the intellectual problems posed by a new awareness of globalisation. The impact of war and the ravages of capitalist industrialisation seem strangely to be present in his work more as a distant backdrop rather than coming to direct focus. By contrast Moltmann's response of faith was initiated in the cataclysm of the Second Word War and the experiences of the bombing of Hamburg, the threat of despair in prisoner-of-war camps and a confronting of the genocide in Nazi death camps. In an almost inexplicable response of hope, Moltmann grappled with the figure of the crucified Jew, Jesus of Nazareth, and the God who raised him from the dead. Moltmann's theological work has taken place *within a globalised world*. He seeks to respond to the blood-letting of the twentieth century, evoked by the names Auschwitz and Hiroshima, by the impact of poverty produced by modern economic systems, and also the human destruction of nature. As a Christian theologian Moltmann speaks of both God's suffering and God's promise to renew the whole creation.

Taking up these themes brings us to the challenge of particularity present in the work of these two theologians. Both appreciate that the Christian community holds to one faith among many. Troeltsch and Moltmann differ in their response to that relationship of the one particular community among the many in quite different ways. Both recognise that the Christian church has spread across the globe and is now present in every culture. Yet for Troeltsch the only possible response to this situation is a 'retreat' (although he does not categorise this negatively) to the Euro-American 'world'. For

Moltmann, the Christian church does not exist for its own sake but is rather to be a sign of the coming reign of God and the coming of the new creation. Both theologians address the question of how the church and its theology may speak of a future for a globalised humanity and the planet itself.

Troeltsch was pressed to develop a new form of historicised Christian theology and church which may find a new form within the critical challenge of modern society to faith and cultic (worship) life. By contrast, he understands the church to be a community called by Jesus Christ into a counter-history of resistance to the powers which oppress and destroy not only human life but threaten all life on the planet. In Moltmann's work then, the challenge of globalisation is whether the church which bears the name Jesus Christ will respond to the call to entrust itself to God who promises the new creation.

Ernst Troeltsch's Response to Historical Plurality

Troeltsch's lifework was an ongoing critique of the attempt to ground Christian theology on absoluteness. Troeltsch opposed apologetic founded either on a 'naïve' or 'artificial' absoluteness because it isolated Christian faith and theology from other forms of life.[1] Troeltsch developed an alternative, seeking to ground Christian theology relatively within cultural life. Trutz Rendtorff[2] correctly points out that Troeltsch saw Christian theology contextually within its European setting. Responding to challenges produced by modern European thought, Troeltsch rejected a solution from 'the East', seeking instead to understand the developing life of Christianity with a solution within its limits. His basic assumption is that Christianity—a contingent, particular historical entity—is inseparable from its relative setting within the stream of the *Religionsgeschichte* (that is, the living reality of religious traditions and cultures). Christianity

---

1. I am following the work of George E Griener in his study of *Ernst Troeltsch and Hermann Schell: Christianity and the World Religions. An Ecumenical Contribution to the History of Apologetics.* European University Studies, Series XXIII Theology, volume 375 (Frankfurt am Main, Berlin, New York, Paris: Peter Lang, 1988).
2. Trutz Rendtorff, 'Europäismus als geschichtlicher Kontext der Theologie. Bemerkungen zur heutigen Kritik a "europäischer" Theologie im Lichte von Ernst Troeltsch', in *Europäische Theologie* (Gütersloh: Gerd Mohn, 1990).

has its place inescapably within the plurality of cultural histories and Christian theology must also find a form to suit.

Troeltsch made the challenge of *historicism* his life's work.[3]. He recognises that the rise of the modern world produced a crisis in Christianity. Natural science coupled with the rise of historical science has removed prior certainties. The 'historical method' has removed any claim that Christianity is absolute. And, more radically, he denies that there can be any access to the absolute in history. Christianity is exposed to the features of historicism, such as relativism, subjectivism. Historical life is inescapably historicised. In his undelivered lecture on ethics and history however, Troeltsch rejects a 'monistic empiricism' which has characterised historicism. He registers the irony that, while empiricism arose in opposition to epistemologies which allowed for a special grounding of Christianity, that same empiricism now denies Christianity a secure or unassailable ground in historical life.

As we consider globalisation, it is clear for Troeltsch that Christian faith, theology and church are located within European culture. Only from here is it possible to engage in the theological task which requires *a priori* a historical rationality as the basis for Christian theology. Here in the European context a *relative ground* may be found for Christian theology. Troeltsch rejects as an abstraction a monolithic concept of 'Christianity', and rejects the Hegelian (Idealist) expectation of progress towards a final unity of religion. Aware of the existence of world religions or cultures, Troeltsch emphasises the individuality of each culture. Each will achieve its own realisation in an unknown future inaccessible to the present, quite separate from the other.

Awareness of differing world cultures leads to a recognition that the culturally conditioned character observed in Christianity is true

---

3. The problems of historicism were detailed in volume 3 of his collected works: *Der Historismus and seine Probleme Gesammelte Schriften, Band 3*, (Tübingen: 1922; reprinted Aalen: 1977); a brief article: 'Die Krisis des Historismus', *Die Neue Rundschau*, 33 (1922); and a series of five unpublished lectures: *Der Historismus und seine Überwinding. Fünf* Vorträge, edited by Friedrich von Hügel, (Berlin: Scientia Verlag, 1924, reprinted Aalen: 1979); English edition: *Christian Thought: Its History and Application,* edited by Baron F. von Hügel (London: University of London Press, 1923). Also (New York: Meridian Books, 1957).

for them—between and within each culture. Thus a singular world history is untenable because history knows nothing of a unified singular development.[4] This involves a 'double relativisation' (within and between) for Christianity, especially as its social forms are intimately related to particular epochs,[5] and have differing forms in those different contexts.

Troeltsch regards each culture as a *sphere;* it follows that each 'sphere of culture' is to be seen in strict separation from the other, and consists of an indissoluble synthesis of culture and religion. Therefore modern Europe (while it is the product of all that has gone to make it up) has now shed its Semitic origins, and is now fully *'de-orientalised, Hellenised and Europacised'*. That is to say, the contemporary form of Christianity is now irrevocably westernised, with its various previous elements absorbed and synthesised.

Christianity is therefore no longer theologically normative for the entirety of human culture and religion—but only for western life and then only as the religion of that particular culture.[6] Any form of differentiation in the field of world religions, such as an assessment of their truth and falsity, or the designation of their character as revealed or natural, disappears. Most significant is the removal of any comparison of other cultures with Christianity. Now Christian theological attention is directed solely within to the development of the plurality of religions, a plurality which is the cultural basis for Europeanism.[7]

---

4. [4] See the entry on Glaube und Geschichte in the theological dictionary, *Religion in Geschichte und Gegenwart*, volume 4 ([Kop-O] 1960), columns 1450-1452, especially 1448 ff.
5. An extended treatment of this appears in *Gesammelte Schriften*, volume I, *Die Soziallehren der christlichen Kirchen und Gruppen.* (Aalen: Scientia-Verlag, *1977; The Social Teaching of the Churches* (London: Allen & Unwin, & New York: MacMillan, 1931; reprinted in two volumes, New York: Harper Torchbook, The Cloister Library, 1960).
6. See 'Die Selbständigkeit der Religion', *Zeitschift für Theologie und K*irche, V and VI (Mohr Siebeck), 1895.
7. In subsequent theological discussion, as illustrated by George A Lindbeck, *The Nature of Doctrine: Religion and Theology in a Postliberal Age* (Westminster Press, Philadelphia, 1984), and Stanley Hauerwas, *Christian Existence Today* (Durham: Labyrinth Press, 1988) and *After Christendom* (Nashville: Abingdon Press, 1991), there is a strong argument being mounted for a postliberal approach which regards Christian theology as exclusive to the Christian community and

Troeltsch's theory of cultural history depends upon an individuality in which the 'history' of each culture consists of unique 'tendencies' which continue until exhausted or transformed. On this basis Troeltsch insisted on the continuing significance of Jesus for Christianity[8] while also allowing for a future dissolution of Christianity itself.[9]

With the concept of '*Europeanism*'[10] Troeltsch seeks to construct a relative, material philosophy of history arising from his rejection of an absolutised universal history and its relativised heir. That construction is undertaken within history, understanding that the goal of history as an absolute end has not been reached—and never will be—*in history*.

'culture'. There is thus a formal similarity to Troeltsch's encircling of Christian theology within the sphere of European culture. While the similarity is a formal one, it also runs the danger of a self-enclosing of Christian theology, and thus isolation from other cultures and world religions. Jürgen Moltmann challenges such self-enclosure by insisting that the horizon of Christian theology is the kingdom of God, thereby refusing such self-enclosure – in work such as *Politische Theologie. Politische Ethik* (Munich: Chr. Kaiser Verlag, & Mainz: Matthias-Grünwald-Verlag, 1984), and *On Human Dignity. Political Theology and Ethics,* translated by Douglas Meeks (London: SCM, 1984). 'Theology for God's sake is always kingdom-of-God theology.' *God for a Secular Society: The Public Relevance of Theology* (London: SCM Press, 1999), 5. Reference to his attitude to theology for the kingdom of God can be found in *Experiences in Theology: Words and Forms of Christian Theology* (Minneapolis: Fortress Press, 2000), Preface, xx and following: 'Theology springs out of a passion for God's kingdom' and thus is a *missionary, public theology.*

8. He argues this in a lecture in 1911: *Die Bedeutung der Geschichtlichkeit Jesu für den Glauben, Schweizer christlichen Studentenkonferenz,* (Tübingen: Scientia Verlag, 1911); and in English: 'The Significance of the Historical Existence of Jesus for Faith', *Ernst Troeltsch's Writings on Theology and Religion,* translated and edited by Robert Morgan and Michael Pye (London: Duckworth and Co, 1977).
9. He faces this possibility in 'Die Zukunftsmöglichkeiten des Christentums', *1910,* volume 2 of his collected works, *Gesammelte Schriften II,* 837–862, especially 840–841.
10. Kondo rightly says Troeltsch's chief work was the 'new definition' (*Neubestimmung*) of Christianity. See Katsuhiko Kondo, *Die Theologie der Gestaltung bei Ernst Troeltsch* (Tübingen: Dissertation in the Faculty of Evangelical Theology, 1977, 26–27), bringing the Christian principle into connection with the modern world in order to open new dynamic possibilities.

Theological Evaluation

Troeltsch employed the 'strategy' of 'Europeanism' as fundamental to his cultural and theological solution in his opposition to absolutist, idealist views which treated European history as 'universal' with a global reach, when 'Europe' was regarded as 'the world' and dominated other cultures. As we noted earlier, that restriction of the European horizon echoed contemporary sentiment. However, Troeltsch's solution found in Europeanism was opposed by those who saw in it a diminution of the 'faith-claim' for Christianity and its missionary task. Within this schema theological method is inextricably associated with its context. In this sense no theology can be 'too contextual'. For Troeltsch the term *history*, in both senses of *research* and *life*, provides that context.

Troeltsch's work anticipated what is now more evident in theological discussion; namely, the question of the relationship between the *one history* confessed by Christian faith and the *many histories* of human culture. This has been taken up extensively in ecumenical discussion under the heading of the 'World Religions'.[11] Such terminology reflects Troeltsch's usage and highlights the enduring significance of his contribution. He identified the tension produced by European global expansion and colonisation and, associated with that, Christian missionary activity.[12] Our current discussion must take into account the global spread of the technocratic culture which originated in Europe and has now spread around the globe affecting all peoples and cultures. The sharpest feature of these developments is internal to Western culture—the church has lost its ascendancy in Western society.

---

11. See for example: Emil Castro, 'The Church and the World of Religions and Cultures: Kraemer in Retrospect', in *The Ecumenical Review*, 41/1 (January, 1989). It demonstrates the shifts and tensions in this discussion.
12. In passing, we note that discussion of secularisation is a key feature of these developments, posed now in current discussion as 'pluralism' and as the 'post-secular' age. Wolfhart Pannenberg in *Christianity in a Secularized World* (London: SCM Press, 1988) provides a brief survey of the issues. Also see Charles Taylor, *The Secular Age* (Harvard: Harvard University Press, 2007). Current discussion challenges the notion that there is an inevitable process which moves from a 'religious world' through to a secularised and de-sacralised age. The literature on this topic is vast.

More recently, another element has been added to these considerations: the recognition of the earth as one planet with humanity participating in one global or ecological system and facing a common threat.[13] Humanity is thus seen to be together with all other planetary life in one global history. Paradoxically this recognition is being accompanied by a re-emergence of many indigenous cultures. Human life consists, therefore, of many different histories. Hegel anticipated this development: a move to universal history would also intensify localisation.[14] I use the term 'global' or 'ecological system' advisedly. The shift to a planetary or global perspective does not necessarily bring with it a consciousness of 'history', and certainly not the progressive or evolutionary history of Idealism. In this complex of issues, however, the eschatological question concerning the unity of the many histories and their future is posed.

Troeltsch's contribution is salient here. He opposed the notion of a duality of histories,[15] and moved from the double-history of received Christian tradition to the single history of the modern historical world view, allowing for only one history with one process, or one development. The monopoly asserted by Christianity over world history was subsequently adopted by modernity. Then, from there, was a recognition of a multiplicity of histories. Ironically, the global expansion which occurred in the name of the 'one' Western history led to an experience of a multiplicity of histories. In other words, due

---

13. J Moltmann, 'Christianity and the World Religions' in *Christianity and the Other Religions*, edited by J Hick (Cambridge: Cambridge University Press, 1980), 191ff.
14. J Moltmann, *Theology of Hope: On the Ground and Implications of a Christian Eschatology*, (London: SCM Press, 1967, German 1965) points out that Hegel in *Rechtsphilosophie* was one of the first to perceive the 'rise of the modern, emancipated society which destroys all the forces of tradition, and to analyse it ... as a "system of needs"' (p.307); 'the age of increasing mass organisation is at the same time dialectically also the age of individuality' (p.309).
15. See Trutz Rendtorff's analysis of Troeltsch's attempt to avoid this duality of history and subsequent discussion in 'Der politische Sinn theologischer Kontroversen. Zur Konvergenz von Widersprüchen im Verhältnis von Religion und Politik', in *Theorie des Christentums* (Tübingen: Stefan Atze, 2006). He regards Troeltsch as the inaugurator of the attempt to speak of revelation, religion and the state without dividing reality. See Trutz Rendtorff, *Historisch-theologische Studien zu seiner Neuzeitlichen* (Gütersloh: Verfassung Gerd Mohn, 1972), 109, 114–15.

to the results of historical research and the experience of European colonial expansion, the monopoly of one was replaced with plurality of the many.[16]

For Troeltsch these multiple cultures and histories remain separate, as read especially in his latest work where he moved decisively away from a future in which these histories merge into one historical Christianity. Indeed, from the one historical method came the recognition of many histories.

The grounds for this view are to be found in Troeltsch's reworked 'eschatology', or lack of it. Troeltsch relativised teleology, already stating in 1911 that the power of the Christian ethos rests in the unfulfillable character of its future. He recognised that the modern world had shifted to '*Diesseits*' (this side), although the 'Beyond' retains its vitalising power. His latest work decisively shifts the Kingdom of God, along with all utopias, to the *Beyond*. Rather than continuity or synthesis between history and the kingdom of God, Troeltsch stresses its discontinuity.[17] This does not concern the result for the soul after death so much as the relationship of the Beyond to history. As Moltmann helpfully observes,[18] if we accept Troeltsch's rejection of European absolutism, both cultural and ecclesiastical, and resist the temptation to set up a general concept of religion, the eschatological question still remains: in what way does the church exercise its vocation *in history* to prepare the way for the coming kingdom of God? In other words, how does the one history of Christian eschatology relate to the plurality of human histories without repeating the mistake of domination on one side or a loss of that distinctive hope on the other? How is the horizon of Christian hope to be expressed?

---

16. See Sarah Coakley, *Christ Without Absolutes: A Study of the Christology of Ernst Troeltsch* (Oxford: Clarendon Press, 1988), 164ff, on the 'many Christs' made possible by radical historicising which produces plurality in theology.
17. Coakley in *Christ without Absolutes*, 90-91 also accurately challenges the accusation that Troeltsch simply identifies the human and the divine in 'pantheism'. She acknowledges that Troeltsch does distinguish between earthly redemption 'and the (eschatological) fullness of redemption'.
18. Moltmann, 'Christianity and the World Religions', 191. See also 202-209 for Moltmann's suggestions for the church as a 'critical catalyst' whose task it is 'to prepare the messianic era among the nations and to make ready the way for the coming redemption, [so] no culture must be pushed out and no religion extinguished'. 'Dialogue' is in the context of 'liberation of the whole creation for the coming kingdom'.

Christian theology subsequent to Troeltsch took up his approach to history as 'one' over against the double history of Protestant Orthodoxy, though harshly critical of Troeltsch and his successors. The single history of modernity thereby set the agenda for subsequent Christian theology.

Notably Troeltsch's commitment to the singularity of history led to an acceptance of plurality. Many cultural histories were to be seen as participating in one human history. However Troeltsch's approach made 'history', as a product of modern Western thought, captive to that culture. In the face of plurality in Western culture, Troeltsch was seeking the means for holding his culture together as one history.

Troeltsch's work illustrates the tension between singular history and plurality or, in Gunton's terms, the one and the many.[19] Recent discussion has witnessed a number of attempts to deal with this relationship of singularity and plurality. However, where these approaches privilege a cultural-plural history over the singularity of Christian faith we are left in a deadlock where one threatens to overwhelm the other.

Here, then, we are left asking a theological question concerning history and the confession of Jesus crucified and risen. When Jesus' resurrection within Jewish salvation-history is taken as the ground for Christian theology, that *particular* event is regarded as primary. Embedded in that event is also the expectation of a *universal* horizon for all human history; one horizon, however, which stands only at the conclusion of history. Therefore, the particularity of the church which lives between these two, may not be foregone.[20] Equally, however, the plurality of the many histories amongst which the church lives must also be acknowledged.[21] Here Moltmann will remind us that in the

---

19. Colin E Gunton, *The One, the Three and the Many: God, Creation and the Culture of Modernity*, 1992 Bampton Lectures (Cambridge: Cambridge University Press, 1993).
20. Dietrich Ritschl proposed this as the future direction of the church in *Memory and Hope: an Inquiry Concerning the Presence of Christ* (New York: Macmillan, 1967), 2: 'We are now returning to the "normal" form of existence, which is that Christians are a minority group among the citizens of the world and that much of what they say is not appreciated by their fellow men (sic). This is the "norm"'.
21. As reflected in ecumenical discussion, *Faith in the Midst of Faiths: Reflections on Dialogue in Community*, edited by S J Samartha (Geneva: WCC, 1977), and the earlier study by Carl F Hallencreutz, *New Approaches to Men of Other Faiths. 1938-1968. A Theological Discussion* (Geneva: WCC, 1970).

'end' of history is in fact (and faith) a new beginning, and the renewal of the whole creation.

Theological consideration of the nature of history demands a response to the 'eschatological' claims made in the Enlightenment, in which modernity was declared to be the final realisation of that history. There Christian theology recalls that human history participates in God's history, in which God is active as both Creator and Redeemer. Where Troeltsch dealt with history in terms of the human capacity to reconstruct the past and construct the future, thus dispensing with absolute claims for any particular history, Christian theology properly takes a substantive interest in the whole of human history interpreted in relation to Jesus the crucified Jew, who was raised from the dead. Christian theology thus engages in an ideology-critique, challenging especially those ideologies which claim absoluteness on the basis of a realised eschatology. Troeltsch was convinced that the entry into that theological task was tightly bound to historical methodology and would thereby provide the means of a new theological response to the modern world. The history he describes has a seriously reductionist character. By contrast, we are much better served by the later theology of Pannenberg and Moltmann which takes the theological task of historical research seriously. By listening carefully to that history, they are also equipped to take up the eschatological character of the history encountered in Jesus Christ.

The Future Promise

In this paper I have sought to show how Troeltsch attempted to establish a relative, cultural ground for Christian theology in the light of the crisis produced by modern historicism and Western theology's encounter with the plurality of human history.

Troeltsch holds that there can be no 'ground' for Christian theology external to history, even more sharply outside European culture. While other theologians have adopted a similar view, they do not accept Troeltsch's self-limitation of Christian theology to modernity's limits. Troeltsch understood very clearly that theology, as defined in modernity, requires an historical ground and sought to provide it, but he did not raise any questions about this demand -enquiring, for example, whether modernity's self–construction is open to question, or whether God's history with Israel and the church has a radical view concerning the inclusion of all nations into that history.

Troeltsch's prior decision to accept the scientific attitude renders him unable to hear the language of promise and hope including all nations and peoples. Here, then, is Troeltsch's appeal to *universality*. But, living as we do in cities where peoples of differing belief and practice are mingled together, Troeltsch's work has a somewhat disembodied and abstract character. His conclusion that an intellectual solution will provide the basis of a theological solution seems strangely detached from the vibrant and lively history he seeks to represent. More seriously, although he insists on the particular character of history (based in his commitment to the empirical), as a theologian Troeltsch loses contact with his unique subject matter, namely the God who by the power of the Spirit raised the crucified Jesus from the dead. He seems to have side-stepped the scandalous claim that God has chosen a particular people with their distinctive history as a means of renewing the whole of humanity.

Again, Troeltsch had strong reasons for resisting the claims of a false universality imposed upon the variegated history of humanity in many cultures around the globe. Regrettably in attempting to hold fast to the plurality of human cultures and their particular histories, it is not clear that he has addressed the relationship of the particular history in which Jesus of Nazareth is found. Rather he insists on the individuality of each culture in such a way as to hermetically seal each from the other.

Considering what this means for Christian theology and life, Troeltsch sees quite accurately the way in which every Christian theology is culturally conditioned. He shows that the task of engaging theologically in history produces a character which is essential to Christian theology. Anticipating Moltmann he expects that it must be involved but in doing so, it risks its own identity.[22] Troeltsch sought to engage Christian theology anew in the world which was breaking up. He recognised that such engagement required new forms of theology. He also sought to protect the identity of Christian theology scientifically, yet even that invited its participation in critical history.

---

22. My observations here have been informed by Moltmann's evocative reflections on the identity and relevance of Christian faith in *The Crucified God* (London: SCM Press, 1972), chapter one.

The substantive question remains for Christian faith and theology which bears witness to a promise made for all peoples and nations. As the bearer of a universal vision based in the promise of God, how can Christianity (learning from a figure such as Ernst Troeltsch) participate fully in human history and cultural life? How will the church acknowledge its place in history as a relative human activity? Understanding that life consists of *particularities*, how will the Christian church be a faithful witness to the Jewish man, Jesus of Nazareth? With Christian theologians, such as Jürgen Moltmann, who have rediscovered the eschatological power of hope, how can the church speak of a global hope for all created life, without seeking to protect its own identity and resisting the urge to impose faith on others? How can the church remain faithful to Jesus Christ crucified and risen with his message of the reign of God that has come near in him, and promises a future in which all barriers, divisions and hatreds—even the power of death itself—will be overcome?

Contributors

Dr Peter Price, is Senior Lecturer at Yarra Theological Union, a College of the University of Divinity, Melbourne, and Adjunct Senior Research Fellow (History) of Monash University School of Philosophical, Historical and International Studies.

Rev Dr Stephen Ames, Chair of the Yarra Institute for Religion and Social Policy Research, Lecturer in the School of Philosophy at Melbourne University. He is also Canon at St Paul's Cathedral, Melbourne.

Rev Dr Bruce Duncan, Senior Lecturer in Moral Theology and History, Yarra Theological Union, Priest of the Redemptorist Order, Executive Director of the Yarra Institute for Religion and Social Policy Research, University of Divinity, Melbourne.

Professor John D'Arcy May, formerly Professor of Interfaith Dialogue at the Irish School of Ecumenics, Trinity College Dublin, and Research Fellow, University of Divinity, Melbourne.

Dr Rowan Ireland, Honorary Associate in the School of Social Sciences and the Institute for Latin American Studies at La Trobe University, Melbourne.

Professor Therese D'Orsa, is Head of Missiology at the Broken Bay Institute, School of Humanities & Social Sciences, University of Newcastle.

Dr James D'Orsa, Conjoint Lecturer, School of Humanities and Social Sciences, University of Newcastle.

Dr Robyn Reynolds, Sister of the Our Lady off the Sacred Heart Congregation, is a Lecturer in Missiology and Spirituality at Yarra Theological Union, University of Divinity, Melbourne.

Rev Dr Wes Campbell, was Uniting Church Chaplain at Melbourne University.